Walking in Purpose & Trusting Divine Timing

DANIELLA CHASE

Becoming Bolder with Every Step
Walking in Purpose & Trusting Divine Timing

Copyright © 2024 Daniella Chase

All Rights Reserved.

Although the author has made every effort to ensure that the information in this book was correct at press time, the author does not assume and hereby disclaim any liability to any party for any loss, damage, or disruption caused by errors or omissions, whether such errors or omissions result from negligence, accident, or any other cause.

No parts of this book may be reproduced in any form or by any electronic or mechanical means, including information storage in retrieval systems, without written permission from the author, except in the case of a reviewer, who may quote brief passages embodied in critical articles or in a review.

ISBN:
979-8-9906769-0-9

Contents

CHAPTER ONE | 1
Can't live with her, can't live without her

CHAPTER TWO | 15
Love Daddy mostest, love Mommy beautiful

CHAPTER THREE | 29
Magic and mischief makers

CHAPTER FOUR | 43
Home and haven

CHAPTER FIVE | 57
A monument more lasting than bronze

CHAPTER SIX | 73
Checkpoint failure, destination success

CHAPTER SEVEN | 83
A leap of faith, a load of courage

CHAPTER EIGHT | 97
Your gifts will make room for you

CHAPTER NINE | 105
Starting a business, building a brand

CHAPTER TEN | 117
You are enough

Dedication

This book is dedicated to the remarkable women whose unwavering love has shaped us, whose enduring strength upholds us, and whose fervent prayers sustain us daily.

In loving memory and eternal gratitude to the angels who have earned their wings:
My Golden Girl CB and Bonus Mother JJ.

Dear Reader,
You are enough.

CHAPTER 1

Can't live with her, can't live without her

Women lead from the front—at least that's what I saw. I first got a bird's eye view of the world while seated on the shoulders of my grandmother or perhaps my mother. Either way, these bold, daring women—the matriarchs who made me—only stood firmly planted because they, too, stood on the foundation of those who preceded them. My maternal grandmother Claudette, or *"CB"* as I fondly call her, is the Grande Dame of our family unit. The adults called her full-mouth Claudette-Beatrice, but ever since my cousin Richard expertly butchered her name into 'beat' and 'rice', his pronunciation has stuck with me.

The cars that drove through our community selling fish and announcing bingo competitions didn't stand a chance next to the loudspeaker my grandmother swallowed. People on the other side of the hill said they could clearly hear her voice. On weekdays, her blare was to ensure all seven rumbustious grandchildren who lived with her completed their chores, dressed, and boarded a minibus for school by 8:30 a.m. One of the ways that my grandmother taught us to be independent was by giving us chores—as soon as I mastered one task, I moved on to learning something new. The boys fed the chickens and collected eggs from the coop. They also raked the leaves from the fruit trees into piles and discarded the plastic shopping bags, which were reused as trash bags. The girls swept and mopped the house and the stairs. The wooden stairs at the back of our house were easier to clean than the front, so I preferred to scrub the back stairs. Most of the time, we agreed to take turns scrubbing the back stairs, but sometimes, I got my hands on the bucket and grabbed the mop before the others, making it a done deal.

    In the mornings before I left for school, CB perched on the wooden armchair in our living room that had long lost its varnish while I sat between her legs on a short plastic stool so she could comb my hair. Monday mornings were dreadful if I didn't detangle my hair, but worse if I was running behind time. Then, my grandmother meticulously inspected each of us from head to toe before giving us the nod of approval to go our way. She rubbed her fingers along my shirt collar, pulled my lips apart to see that I had brushed my teeth and glanced at my feet to see that my socks and shoes were spick and span. If I passed her inspection, she would give me pocket money and I would skip out the door. If I didn't, she would send me to get it right before returning to her. Amusingly, my grandmother's marching orders were conveyed either through the most comprehensive gaze that my sense could perceive—or at times, through petrifying but equally effective commands issued with her swishing wrist and wand-like fingers.

On weekends, CB's blare was used religiously to ensure we were prepared and ready for our timely dispatch to church—twice, if possible. Most Sundays, we attended once in the morning and again in the afternoon. My grandmother's policy was non-negotiable when it came to church and school. I was not exempt unless I had asthma, diarrhoea, or a roasting fever. If I couldn't find my hair bobbles, she hurriedly styled my hair with six or so plaits, if I couldn't find my church socks—which were white with frills—I wore my shoes without any, if the buses were on strike, I walked. My grandmother quoted the scripture, *"Render your heart and not your garment"* enough times for me to refrain from expressing any dissatisfaction with how she combed my hair or my preference to stay at home rather than wear my shoes without socks. By hook or by crook, I went to church and school. For someone who never went to church, CB was adamant that we should never miss a Sunday's service. Whenever I asked why she didn't accompany us, she responded,

BECOMING BOLDER WITH EVERY STEP

"God knows my heart!". I was often tempted to ask how I could get God to know my heart, too, so I could stay at home and play with my dolls. I assumed CB and God had their heart-to-heart early in the mornings when she sat on the edge of her bed to read the Holy Bible and the Our Daily Bread booklet before she did anything else.

The journey to the church on Sunday mornings was about a fifteen-minute walk—at least when measured by adult steps. But for us, where the unit of distance was relative to adventure, the same journey often became a 30-minute-long trek—complete with its own shortcuts, barbed-wire fenced obstacle course, and public fruit trees that we subjected to our brutal gang raids. Whenever we finally arrived, the Sunday School service was led by the gentle giant, Sister Miriam, in a small concrete structure with no windows; only two rows of design blocks which air passed through and the sign of the cross painted above the front door. Sister Miriam's church wasn't like any of those grandiose churches I saw on TV with dazzling chandeliers, cushioned seats and ornate pulpits. Instead, her church had long wooden pews that hurt my buttocks when I sat for too long, a keyboard which was only played by Sister Miriam's husband, a tambourine missing some of its jingles and a rusty old fan that made more noise than it blew cool air.

As I recall, my favourite thing about the morning services was always the stories Sister Miriam told us about

Jesus—like how He turned water into wine and caused an uproar at that temple. Her stories were more than words. For each story, she hung a piece of fabric over a chalkboard and then added paper stickers of the scenes and characters; each character appearing and disappearing as she told the story.

The Sunday School service in the afternoon was not held in a church. Our Sunday School teachers borrowed rooms from the school next door, or we simply sat outside. However, unlike the morning service, this was deeply Baptist so there was thunderous clapping to riveting songs like *"Satan is a sly old fox, if I catch him I'll lock him in a box"*. But these songs weren't my favourite part of the service. My favourite part was getting gift boxes donated by the Samaritan's Purse. Those Samaritan's Purse induced my unfailing attendance in the scorching sun or pouring rain. They were like getting a gift from your favourite uncle or aunt who lived in America, where everything could be found. In one of my boxes, I received a figurine of Moses. He was a white man with curly hair, wrapped in cloth, and held a stick like the one we used to pick sugar apples. Whenever I pressed the button on his back, he uttered one of the Ten Commandments. Receiving my Samaritan's Purse was also the only time I didn't care that the service took an hour of my playtime.

But CB didn't care a thing—or *one ass*, as she would say, about how I preferred to spend my Sundays. Her priority was ensuring we were never hungry, indisciplined, or sick. She taught us that there was a difference between being rude and being vocal. She encouraged us to be vocal, but she never tolerated rudeness. We greeted everyone we passed along and were reminded to use the magic words *'please'* and *'thank you'*. *"Manners maketh man!"* was one of her common phrases. My grandmother's discipline and protection went hand in hand. One way to tempt fate would be to threaten our safety.

Once, there was a man called *"Parachute"*—my cousins took it up from everyone else. Whenever he passed by our house on his way home, they would loudly call out *"Parachute!"* before doubling over with laughter. Their taunts infuriated him, so much so that he slurred expletives as he rode past. One afternoon, when Parachute had finally had it up to his neck with my cousins' taunts, he pushed his bicycle up the hill to our house and lodged his complaint against my cousins. CB agreed that the boys were out of line, but Parachute took God out of his thoughts when he threatened to *"do something to them"* the next time they taunted him. The very next day, CB joined my cousins on a makeshift bench below the hill where we lived and waited for Parachute to pass. As he approached, she told the boys to call out for him so she could find out what was the *"something"* he intended to do. Upon realising he didn't have my grandmother's support, Parachute humbly continued his journey. Nonetheless, CB warned the boys to desist from their name-calling.

For CB, it has always been family first, then education. She didn't waste the chance to let anyone know that she would never throw away her bad for anybody else's good. Before we could read for ourselves, she read stories to us. Whenever I encountered words I couldn't pronounce, I ran to CB for aid. She was my Thesaurus. She made me practise spelling challenging words like Uitvlugt—the Dutch-origin name of a coastal village that entangled spelling bee champions year after year on TV. Sometimes, we gathered around her to solve the riddles from the Sunday newspapers and listen to Guyanese fables about Sensi Bill & Stupidy Bill and stories of good ole' Anansi.

Even so, she never spared the rod to spoil any of us. My grandmother's rod of correction could be a plastic hair comb, hairbrush, wooden ruler, metal spoon, a twig from a fruit tree, or whatever object was within her reach. If ever I decided to run, her response was daring. *"Give God your soul and give me your behind when I catch you"*. And sure enough, she always caught me. Sometimes I managed to avoid the rod early in the day and hoped that CB would forget it by evening. What a dotish mistake! CB had a way of catching me right after a bath when I was naked and damp. She snuck up behind me, and as soon as I felt the sting, I knew it was from my earlier misdemeanour. Somehow, the delayed cut-ass always felt like it included extra heat for outrunning her, but that didn't stop me from running every time.

BECOMING BOLDER WITH EVERY STEP

On the weekends, CB also baked. Our oven was a recycled metal barrel in the backyard that she fired up using charcoal. During the preparatory stage of mixing the flour, I recall always asking for pieces of dough so I could mimic her kneading motion. If there was space in the pan, I baked my miniature bread, too. It was an honour to be allowed to pour the water into the bowl while she mixed the flour, using her average instead of referring to one of the many recipe books she had accumulated. In my mind, being allowed to pour the water automatically promoted me to her baking assistant, with assumed responsibility for the quality of the bread. I poured it carefully to ensure it was the exact amount that she needed. When the dough had stayed in the oven for the proper time, she brought out her pans of perfectly golden-brown loaves to cool on our dining table. If she was up to it, she grated coconuts and baked coconut buns or made us sugar cake.

In retrospect, I don't know how much time my grandmother had available for herself, considering the amount of time she spent taking care of us. I suppose that's why she sent us to church twice. She did everything for us and asked for only two things in return: to pluck out her grey hairs and to scratch her head. What now seem to be small and reasonable adult requests felt quite the opposite as a child. I felt as though CB always chose the most inconvenient time to make these requests—during the days when I wanted to gallivant around or at nights when I was exhausted. Whenever she asked me, I would complain that there were too many grey hairs to pluck or that my hands were weary from scratching her dandruff. The only time I did not complain about being in her hair was when I wanted to accessorise it with my hair bobbles and ribbons or when she offered to pay me.

CB always gave her best, often giving everything she had. If someone CB considered stingy gave her money, she did not spend it immediately. She tucked it between the pages of her Bible saying, *"Lord, bless this lil money."* Many months could go by before CB came across the money, and when she did, she lit up with surprise. *"God don't come, but He does send!"* she'd exclaim before spending the money. When she got her first washing machine, it took months for her to use it regularly. No discourse on the convenience that the new machine promised could persuade my grandmother to abandon her preference for hand-washing each garment. Her stubbornness didn't change even after my brother, Otis, bought her a touchscreen smartphone. CB dismissed the phone as *'a stupid little thing without buttons'*. Yet, once she got accustomed to it, she watched home remedy videos on YouTube and reconnected with many of her friends on Facebook and WhatsApp.

While many of my grandmother's friends migrated to foreign, they kept in touch by writing letters to each other. In their letters, CB and her friends mostly shared details about their spouses and children—who had completed their studies, got married or had a baby, their jobs, or their next planned trip to Guyana. Sometimes they asked CB if she wanted anything when they visited, and her favourite things to ask for were word search puzzle books and pancake syrup. I know this because I went into her box of letters and read them. Don't judge me—I was inquisitive!

We were often told, *"When big people talking, lil children must disappear"* so when any adult visited our home, that was my indication to run off into the yard and play. Sometimes, though, they became so caught up in their stories that they forgot I was right next to them and on those occasions, I was all ears. If I was caught eavesdropping, CB gave me a sharp cut-eye and I skedaddled without hesitation, fearing she might scold me for listening to 'big people business'.

CB cooked every meal, cleaned our home and ironed every piece of clothing, yet she never missed any meetings at our schools. She was familiar with all our teachers. If there was anything she wasn't too sure of, she wrote a note and slipped it into our haversacks. At the start of every school semester, she sat for hours at the dining table to wrap our book covers with paper and warned us to keep them tidy. When completing homework and projects, she never dropped the ball. Regardless of the task, CB helped us get it done. If there was a concept that was unfamiliar to her—that's where our neighbour, Teacher June, came in. Teacher

CAN'T LIVE WITH HER, CAN'T LIVE WITHOUT HER

June and CB had many conversations over the barbed wire fence separating our houses. They talked about the news, people in the government, school projects we needed help with and other things that they leaned in too close for me to hear. Their daily conversations lasted until Teacher June ran off for work and CB resumed our preparation for school.

On one occasion, I overheard Teacher June telling CB that the hearse transported the dead man. I was flabbergasted that a horse was used to carry a dead man's body and curiously intervened on the animal's behalf. When Teacher June asked me to spell the word, I confidently spelt, *"H-O-R-S-E"*, and they both burst out with laughter before teaching me the difference. Did that stop me from listening to their conversations? Absolutely not!

While I'm sure all our neighbours kept an eye on us whenever CB wasn't around, Teacher June was the one I went to in an emergency—even when the crisis was helping me throw a surprise for CB's birthday. Whenever my grandmother wasn't at home, my siblings, cousins and I put on a show—dressing in her clothes and imitating some of the things she said and did. For instance, if we were looking for the pencil sharpener we misplaced and asked my grandmother if she knew where it was, she would jokingly respond that she saw it walking down the street earlier in the day. Or when we asked her where to put our books, which had their designated place on the bookshelf, she would indicatively tug at her dress.

Perhaps the worst thing I've done in my grandmother's absence is congregate with my siblings and cousins behind our bathroom in the backyard to smoke. My cousin, Richard rolled up a piece of newspaper stuffed with some dried grass while we stood waiting in a circle. He confidently used the box of matches to set it alight. He took the first puff, passed it around and told us to do the same. *"Gently, pull"* he instructed. But when our faux cigarette reached me, I wrapped my lips around the paper, sucked my jaw and pulled so strongly that I started choking and shoved the piece right back into Richard's hand before running off to wash the burning sensation from my throat. When CB returned home, it was as if nothing had ever happened.

My grandmother's blare is no longer to prepare me for school or send me off to church, but our home is no less noisy than it was as a child. Unless there's a power outage, CB's radio comes on daily by 6 a.m. without fail. If it were up to her, I would still have to fill a bucket with water and mop the stairs every morning. Though she no longer picks a twig from the fruit tree to give me *"a good cut-ass"*, her piercing eyes serve as a steady reminder that her authority remains intact. Despite the many changes, CB continues to lavish me with love, impart wisdom—though sometimes wrapped with colourful language—and provide guidance.

At every milestone, she celebrates with me and reminds me of the power and purpose I carry within. I am forever indebted to my grandmother for nurturing and moulding the bold woman I was yet to become.

BECOMING BOLDER WITH EVERY STEP

I CARRY WITHIN ME
THE *power*
TO ACHIEVE
great things

CHAPTER 2

Love Daddy mostest, love Mommy beautiful

My parents had young love. From the stories they shared, it was a hot, steaming romance until it wasn't. My father, a natural-born explorer, dived into the matters of the heart and discovered his treasure, while my mother was head over heels for him. I am proof of their love, one of the three gems in the crown of their creation. Otis, the firstborn, was named after my father. I was born two years later, and my sister Youkona was born two years after me. Six years later, my mother gave birth to my baby sister, Keshauna, completing our collection.

Though both my parents were mostly away from our home during my younger years, their absence felt very different. My father would call on the telephone, but I wouldn't see him. Sometimes, I'd receive a call from him on my birthday, but there were times when the year would go by without any calls from him at all. Whenever he telephoned, I felt such an overwhelming rush that eclipsed every other emotion. I naïvely asked, *"Daddy, when are you coming home?"*, and he always responded, *"Soon, Darling. Soon!"*.

I don't remember much of my parents' relationship except for what was likely the end of it and one of the scariest days of my life. From the yard where I was riding my bicycle, I heard their raised voices at each other. I wasn't paying close attention, but CB who knew all too well what usually followed, stood on the back stairs with her ears cocked. Without another word, Mommy made a sudden dash into the yard and sprinted towards the front gate while Daddy chased behind her.

CB's screams rang out but it wasn't long before Daddy caught up and they rumbled and tumbled among the trees in the gully at the bottom of the hill where we lived. My screams did nothing to stop my father and by the time our neighbours managed to pull Mommy away, she was already beaten to a pulp. I worriedly wondered whether Mommy was alive the rest of that day—which felt like forever. It wasn't until I felt her lying in bed beside me that my fears were allayed. I rubbed my hands across her body to ensure I wasn't dreaming, and she flinched when my fingers touched her forehead, where she wore a bandage.

LOVE DADDY MOSTEST, LOVE MOMMY BEAUTIFUL

After that day, I didn't see my father or hear from him for a long time. Then, out of the blue, he appeared in the front of our yard. He and Mommy talked for a few minutes before she dressed us and packed our bags for us to spend the holiday in the city with our father. Our holidays in the city were exciting—it meant a long speed boat ride, then a longer bus ride, passing big glass stores with many nice things on display, seeing the Cuffy statue, going to the zoo and eating KFC. Our holiday lasted for only a few days, then my father left again—this time, as I recall, for eight years.

Most of the things I knew about my father were the stories I heard from others. His sister, Aunt Gilleon, told me stories of their childhood about how fearless Daddy had been. I heard stories of his adventures as a diver in the treacherous Mazaruni River and his wealth of knowledge about diamonds and other gemstones. Mommy told me stories about the way my father enjoyed combing my hair, giving me baths and changing my nappies. She told me how much he loved playing Scrabble—making up words that don't exist, and his dream of seeing the Panama Canal. She never talked about their fights and greatly detested my grandmother's rants.

When I learnt to write letters, my parents were the first people to whom I sent them. Every time I knew of someone travelling to the community where my father lived, I wrote a letter identical to the template I learnt at school and requested my letter be delivered.

'Dear Dad,

How are you? I hope you are in the best of health. As for me, I am fine, thank you. I am writing this letter to tell you...'

I wrote about how much I scored on my tests, my friends, and whatever else I could think of writing. Then, I asked him when he was coming home as I always did. On each envelope, I wrote the words:

'Written with a pen and sealed with a kiss—God bless my father's hands as he opens this.'

I memorised those words from snooping through my older cousin Whitney's little green book that she thought was secretly stashed from us on a shelf between some school textbooks. Whenever I sent my letter, I eagerly awaited my father's response. I saw how CB wrote letters to her friends who lived abroad, asking them questions and responding to theirs, so I understood how sending and receiving letters worked. Not receiving any letters from my father made me wonder if he ever received mine.

Coincidentally, eight years after I'd last seen my father, our church's annual trip was confirmed to visit

Imbaimadai—an Indigenous mining community where he lived. When he telephoned, I told him about the possibility of us visiting him, and he committed to financing the trip. I was so excited, but he never called again. By the time the trip came around, I had lost all desire to see my father. Yet, Mommy insisted that it was a much-needed opportunity for us to bond with our father, so she financed our trip—showing far more enthusiasm than any of us had. If my father loved us, he would come home—I thought. But Mommy was confident that any resentment I felt towards my father would dissipate as soon as we were together.

When Otis, Youkona and I arrived in Imbaimadai, there was no sign of our father. *None. Zilch!* During the days when Otis and Youkona went off to Bible Study sessions with the rest of the group, I sat on the stairs of the building where we stayed. Whenever someone passed by, I asked if they recognised my father, or knew where his mining operation was located. I checked in on every available radio frequency—near and far, searching for him without luck. Then, two days before our return flight to Georgetown, I left a message for my father on one of the radio frequencies, letting him know that if he did not desire to see us, he should have explicitly said so. Still, after we'd flown more than one hundred and sixty miles behind God's back to see him, he needed to refund our mother's money for his eye-pass. My mother didn't demand a refund. I—the usual mouthpiece for my siblings—did. The next day, my father left specific instructions. He instructed me to hire a boat with my siblings along with his mother to take us to Kamarang—another Indigenous mining community approximately 41 km away, where he would meet us.

I made the arrangements with a man who knew my father and he agreed to collect his payment upon our arrival at Kamarang. We packed our georgie bundles and were ready to skedaddle. Under the unforgiving gaze of the Mazaruni sun, we spent the next day travelling from Imbaimadai to Kamarang in a small, wooden motor-powered boat that seemed to move no faster than the pace of the water current. We arrived at approximately 4 p.m.—tired, scorched and famished. As the boat pulled into the shore, a man stood beside the river bank clad in a forest green t-shirt, khaki cargo shorts and Clarks shoes. I didn't recognise him. His mother first spotted him and shouted all of his names. When we disembarked the vessel, my father's words were, *"Y'all geh big. If I di see y'all on the road, I woulda pass y'all straight"*, meaning that we'd grown beyond his recognition. *"Puppy does turn dog"*, I wanted to tell him but held my tongue. When he offered to carry my suitcase, I declined. I shook his hand and proceeded up a hill and across an open field towards the hotel where he indicated we were staying.

The first few hours were filled with silence and the urge to ask a million questions, but Youkona broke the silence. In her usual matter-of-fact approach, she told him about the countless times we had waited for him to come home and how much his broken promises hurt. She told him how hard Mommy worked and how much she sacrificed to make up for his absence. My father silently stared at us, and his silence irritated me. I wanted him to apologise—or say something. He did neither.

He took us to the river for a bath, then we returned to the hotel for dinner, by which time good-humoured conversations began to flow. We talked about the days we spent in Imbaimadai and how I followed a complete stranger into the savannahs in my quest to find him. Then we moved to stories about when we were toddlers—with all our little antics. Mommy was right about Daddy's wittiness. By the night's end, Youkona and I were cradled in our father's arms, wholly lovestruck and enjoying his stories about when we were younger.

My father's mental album hadn't been updated since the last time we spent that holiday together, and he had so many stories of when we were babies—stories I was hearing for the first time. He told us that before I learnt how to pronounce my name correctly, I pronounced it *"La-leH-la"* and said, *"I love Mommy beautiful and I love Daddy mostest"*. Allegedly, I was a 'Daddy's girl' before I could remember and fought with my siblings for my father's undivided attention. My father told each story with dates and timestamps in a way I thought only my brother was capable of doing.

Everyone in Kamarang who knew my parents while they were a couple exclaimed how big we'd grown from the last time they saw us. *"Otis, this is the big boy?"* Daddy beamed with pride, affirmatively nodding his head. *"This one is the baby that was in she mother belly?"*. Again, he shook his head to let them know they were spot on. *"Yes, she look just like she mother and the baby look just like you!"*, they added, shifting their glances between me and Youkona with wide smiles.

In the evenings, Daddy prepared dinner, and we played the game of Scrabble that Mommy insisted we carry on the trip. He loved it as much as she said he would, beating us terribly in each game. Spending time with my father revealed a side of him I never knew and gave me new memories to cherish. The days we spent together were euphoric and some of the best days of my life. I fell asleep to the sound of his lullabies, woke up in his arms, and spent the day foot and foot behind him in the mining pit prospecting and mining for the diamonds with which I intended to return.

Before our trip to Kamarang, Daddy didn't speak about Mommy. Yet, while we were with him, he remarked about the traits I inherited from her. He talked about how much he loved the sound of my laughter, which echoed hers and that her *"mud toes"* and mine were alike. Whenever I asked him about their relationship, he quickly redirected the conversation. If ever I fussed over anything, he hushed me, saying, *"Let not your heart be troubled, Darling"*— or another of his many parables. During one of our conversations, my father recited: *"Written with a pen, sealed with a kiss—God bless my father's hands as he opens this"* and asked me if those words sounded familiar. As soon as he said them, I felt a rush of emotions—disappointment, anger and hurt.

Beyond the confirmation that my father had received at least one of my letters, that moment was an excruciating reminder of the rejection I felt in the many years I hadn't seen, or heard from him, and of all his broken promises to come home. It was difficult for me to reconcile his actions with what he displayed during the short trip—intelligence, deep faith and unadulterated affection.

Mommy, too, was away from our home for weeks, but I always believed she would return as soon as possible. That was one of the promises she made each time. Before entering a trade in the far-flung gold mines that necessitated her absence, she awoke at the crack of dawn to set up the trolley and stock of fish she sold on foot. Later, she operated a stall at the local market selling clothing, footwear, ornaments and storybooks. While Mommy was gone, I wrote letters to her, too. One of my most precious memories is her first reply, which began with the words:

BECOMING BOLDER WITH EVERY STEP

'My Dearest Daniella'

In her letter, Mommy told me how happy she was to receive my letter, how proud she felt, how much she dreaded being so far away, how soon we would be reunited and made corrections to any misspellings in my letter. I understood my mother's absence as a sacrifice she made for me and my siblings. There was sadness when she left but inexplicable joy every time she returned.

And when she returned, her presence filled our home with life. Her thunderous voice rang out from the bathroom, belting out Skyline Pigeon by Elton John. Although, Elton himself might have been surprised that it was his song she sang—given her unique rendition. Mommy's singing, though off-key yet powerful, brought a sense of normalcy and comfort. It was a reminder that despite the long hours she spent away working, her heart was always with us.

While CB and Mommy were disciplinarians alike, my mother had the advantage of agility. She ran behind me so her admonitions weren't delayed. On one occasion, I saw her approaching me and made the quickest dash into the yard. We went on a high-speed chase—down the stairs and around the yard. Unsurprisingly, I cultivated my stardom in the 100-metre race at school by the speed I ran from my mother and grandmother's beatings. Our yard was my track and if they intended to beat me, they had to catch me first.

Mommy chased me around the yard until the gap grew too wide and she was out of breath. Then she stood with her hands on her akimbo, chuckled and said, *"Hog been ask e momma, 'Wah mek ya mouth so long?. He seh, Picknee, you day a come'"*. My mother, too, ran from CB's beatings as a child.

'Best Dancer of the Family' and 'Mommy' are two of the titles my mother holds dearly. Whether chutney, soca or reggae music, Mommy lets loose to the rhythm. That's the reason CB calls her a *"whining sensation"*. CB has told the story many times when Mommy as a young girl ran into the streets and jumped in front of the passing Mashramani National Costume Parade Band. Mommy, as CB recounted, danced to her heart's contentment, then merrily returned to the house as if she had not just turned everybody's head and held up the band. Whenever CB told the story, Mommy proudly agreed. But as my luck would have it, this isn't one of her traits that I inherited. Whenever I danced, CB teased that my waist would do well with some engine oil.

On a separate occasion, I heard one of my mother's friends refer to her by *"Bennamup"*—a nickname. So, the next time she called out for me, I responded, *"Yes, Bennamup!"*, instead of my usual *"Yes, Mommy"*. My mother didn't need to say a word when she spun around to look straight at me. Her glance which was sharp enough to cut me, simultaneously conveyed her shock and a stern warning that I was never to do that again.

BECOMING BOLDER WITH EVERY STEP

When it came to education, it was my mother's way or—as she often reminded us—the highway. Her way was that we had to excel in our studies. This constituted her reward for her sacrifices. The *'highway'* was a daring place I never ventured. While my mother missed most of my birthdays, school meetings and athletic championships due to work, she never missed any of my graduation ceremonies. My graduation ceremonies always doubled as hers. She wore her prettiest dress and took more photos than the official event photographer. In all her voluptuous glory, Mommy smoothly weaved through the crowd and captured our photos on her Canon camera. She erupted in cheers and applause every time my name echoed through the public address system. Her smile was always the biggest and brightest in the room with all the other graduates and their guests. We repaid Mommy's sacrifices with stellar grades, and she rewarded those achievements with books.

Mommy made sacrifices that went unnoticed and unacknowledged. She did whatever was required and I knew it was all for us. I watched her fearlessly navigate James Brown's *A Man's World* with resilience, strength and intuitiveness. With unflinching determination, she hopped into boats, mounted trucks and flew across the country to dangerous and unfamiliar territories. When the generator that powered electricty to our home stopped working, she sat for hours with all her tools before her—dismantling and reassembling it until it was fixed.

It was the same when the television, stereo set, water pump, and everything else in our home malfunctioned.

My first trip to one of the gold mining communities where Mommy operated a general store was against her wishes, but I was determined as usual. When I saw the sailor skillfully navigate the rapids and ride the waves that slammed against our boat, I knew I'd be indomitable if I only inherited half of Mommy's strength and a quarter of her fearlessness. Countless times, I've asked my mother how she does it all and her response is always, *"Only God knows!"*. I have never gone to a place where my mother's prayers haven't gone before me. My mother created a world that allowed me to dream and then taught me to dream boldly.

BECOMING BOLDER WITH EVERY STEP

MY DREAMS ARE

limitless

CHAPTER 3

Magic and mischief makers

As a child, every day held opportunities for magic and mischief. With seven or more children together, our days were brimming with both. Growing up with my grandmother, my childhood was an endless adventure fueled by curiosity and boundless imagination. As soon as CB took her eyes off us, we were up to some tomfoolery. We used our pencils to unravel the cassettes and raced to see who could reel them in fastest. If we couldn't reel them in, we hid them behind the player. When CB discovered the cassettes and asked who unravelled them, I was quick to shout, *"I don't know, granny!"*. *"Then it was Mr Nobody"*, she told us and reeled in the cassettes. As my grandmother said time and time again, *"Mischief don't got owner"*.

BECOMING BOLDER WITH EVERY STEP

In the front of our yard, we drew hopscotch grids in the sand, our nimble feet hopping from square to square. Some afternoons, our neighbours' children who were around the same age as us came over, and it was the more the merrier. We transformed empty milk tins into stilts, our hearts racing with excitement as we balanced precariously above the ground. Those empty milk tins became the passports to our imagination, and we soared high above the earth, one wobbly step at a time. We had games lined up one after the other. *"One, two, three—red light, statue!"*, I called out at the top of my voice while I stood at the front gate with my back turned to the others bolting towards me. Then, when I spun around, everyone stood still as a statue and didn't move until my back was turned again. The first person who took possession of the stick in my hand took my place. When we had enough of that, we moved on to play freeze and melt or hide and seek—squeezing ourselves into every possible hiding spot. We often fell out over who counted too fast or who peeped to see where the others were hiding. Yet, despite those fallouts, in a split second, we were as thick as thieves again.

One fateful afternoon, curiosity led me under the bottom of the house, where I found a forgotten jar of green paint. I twisted the lid until I got it opened and, in doing so, released a cascade of emerald chaos. The paint splattered all over me, staining my clothes and skin. Panicking, I tried to clean myself with my already paint-smeared hands, but it only made the situation messier. I looked like a big clump of green moss, so I ran to the nearby pipe, hoping the water would wash away my colourful sins. But the stubborn, oil-based paint clung to me like a tick and I ended up going straight to CB for help. Thankfully, she was in a good mood. She took one look at my paint-splattered predicament and just shook her head. With her gentle touch and the patience only my grandmother could muster, she scrubbed away the vibrant evidence of my calamity and reminded me of another one of the proverbial expressions she always had at the tip of her tongue—*"Fast fly does stick up in cow BT hole!"*.

With mischief integral to our daily lives, we always found a way around the rules that our adults made. My cousin Richard, the usual ringleader, once attempted a magic trick with a lighter. *"Again, again, again!"*, we shouted—thoroughly entertained. Before he could *"Abracadabra!"* us a third time, the lighter exploded when he struck the wheel. In a panic, the fake magician flung the lighter into an armchair close by and the chair caught fire. Luckily for us, we quickly extinguished the blaze, but that cost Richard his credibility as a magician and a sound reprimand from my aunt. Playing with fire and firecrackers was a serious *no-no*. Yet, each spark set off fireworks in our minds, and we did the opposite of what we were told.

During the rainy season, the potholes in the roads became Olympic-sized pools and fewer buses traversed the roads. When this happened, it became difficult to get a minibus in the mornings so we walked to school. I detested walking to school. It was an almost three-mile walk, and by the time I arrived at school, I was sweaty. Under my arms felt prickly like there was a big branch full of plimpas from the kuru tree. Worse yet, if I was late, our Head Teacher would be standing in front of the gate with her mouth pursed up ready to administer the most stinging lashes to the palm of my hands.

But the rainy season didn't inconvenience Mr Andrew who drove a big Bedford truck which had a canopy for shelter. Mr Andrew transported students who lived in distant villages to their respective schools so on one occasion we pleaded with him for a ride. However, he sat high and mighty in his truck, as if he were a king on his throne, denying our request. He would soon learn the saying that goes *'the stricter the government, the wiser the population'* because our ringleader was always quick to hatch a cunning plan. Richard proposed that we wait at the pedestrian crossing near our home, strategically timed to coincide with Mr Andrew's customary stop for students to disembark.

The plan was simple yet perilous—as Mr Andrew halted his truck, we would climb onto the ladder affixed to the rear. Any misstep and we risked getting into serious trouble, either by being caught or falling from the truck. If CB only turned into a bird and saw what we were up to, woe be unto our souls; as no jim cock bring ram goat story would save us. So, with our hearts racing in our chests, we awaited the following day to execute our daring plan. We scrambled aboard the truck that first morning before Mr Andrew shifted gears and arrived at school safe and sound. Doing that fueled our flame, and we kept on doing it. However, when fewer students were disembarking another morning, I was making my way up when the truck wheels started rolling. Fear gripped me as I held on to the ladder with a million thoughts flashing across my mind—would I die if I fell from the truck? Would I even tell my grandmother if I survived the fall? Thankfully, Richard quickly pulled me but that was the last day I ever set foot into Mr Andrew's truck.

Hopping onto Mr Andrew's truck, or walking to school meant having extra money in our pockets—and extra money meant buying ring-sweeties or going to the game shop—for my cousins—without asking our grandmother. Richard's brother, David, was the mastermind of our cash plans and always had a trick up his sleeve. He learnt that the minibus conductors preferred bills over coins as fares. So, he converted his bills to coins every day before boarding the bus. When he offered them the coins, they just waved him off without taking his money and he walked off skinning his teeth like a roasted dog. But he was too steady with his trickery and when the conductors caught on to what he was doing, they started taking those same coins from him.

BECOMING BOLDER WITH EVERY STEP

On Sundays, our church offering provided another opportunity for mischief. To each of us, CB gave forty dollars for offering and an extra twenty dollars for snacks. However, the money for snacks wasn't guaranteed. Sometimes, it was only the forty dollars for an offering. When the offering basket came around to us, David waited last to put his money. Then, when he did, he slipped only twenty of the forty dollars CB had given to him and kept the next twenty to buy snacks on our way home. The little scamp ran ahead of us, eager to execute his plan, bought himself an icicle and didn't even share a lick with us despite our pleas. As soon as we got home, we ranted to CB about what David had done—purely out of jealousy. However, that day I learnt to kill two birds with one stone as well.

My cousins and I attended different schools, so I had my own adventures of *Gypsy in the moonlight* and *Chi-Chi Chi-Chi Bum-Bum* with my friends. When school was dismissed in the afternoons, my friends and I made our way to the bustling park. Although my school was just a few corners away, I always relished the walk with my friends. Our little group included Kerry who was the first to reach her home, followed by Varsha who made her stop at her father's DVD shop and then Lloyd and I were the last to get a minibus to take us to our homes. Amidst our lively conversations, we exchanged greetings with everyone we encountered along the way.

At one end of the shopper's arcade, there was Ms Lizzie with her crimson red hair in a pixie cut and Ms Roxanne, each running a clothing boutique. Opposite their stalls was Aunty Ann, sitting outside her confectionery store that boasted an ice cream cone machine. Aunty Ann wasn't my real aunt, but addressing any adult full-mouth as a child was an abominable act. Then, we couldn't forget the tailor, easily identifiable by the slim measuring tape draped around his neck and the oversized scissors he wielded. If he happened to be engrossed in sewing, I'd reserve my greetings for his brother, whose grocery shop was diagonally across the street.

On the opposite end of the arcade, more shops beckoned with their tempting displays of shoes and clothing. We encountered a young goldsmith plying his trade and a woman who, in the afternoons, set up her mobile cart with delectable snacks that I could smell from a mile away. People flocked around her to get a taste of her channa, egg balls, meatballs, pholourie and souse. If I had any money by the time I reached the park, I bought white pudding and asked for her mango sour to be lavishly poured on top of it.

However, passing the men who sold clothing was always a less pleasant experience. They would tease me as I approached, calling me *"ugly"* to provoke a reaction. Although I tried not to be deterred, I swiftly freed my hands of whatever I held; whether it was my umbrella or water bottle. With a confident click of my fingers and a defiant roll of my eyes, I retorted, *"Sticks and stones may break my bones, but words will never hurt me."* Yet, deep down, they knew their taunts could still elicit a response, no matter how determined I was to stand my ground.

When I finished clicking my fingers and giving them a sharp cut-eye, I dashed to catch a minibus that was not too overloaded. Sometimes, during the rush hour, there might be only one bus and I squeezed into a seat like sardine in a tin with six or eight other children. If I were lucky, one or two of them would reach their homes before I shouted over the music, telling the driver, *"Stop at the wooden bridge on the left"* as the bus approached my home. As soon as I arrived home, I regrouped with my siblings and cousins, picking up from where we'd left off.

As the saying goes, '*When the cat's away, the mice will play*'. Sure enough, we played by different rules in my grandmother's absence. We made swimming pools from the plastic barrels she used to store water. There were enough barrels for us to each have one to ourselves, and we played for hours on end; sometimes forgetting that we had our chores to complete. When the black tanks that collected rainwater overflowed, they became our shower. If it ever rained while the sun peeked through the clouds, we chanted *"rain falling, sun shining, satan and he wife fighting"*, amid laughter.

One afternoon, CB returned home earlier than we'd expected and every man Jack, except my cousin Claudia, bolted helter-skelter like our lives depended on it—because they did. Claudia dived into the barrel and tried to hold her breath but by the time she poked her head up for air, CB's big hands snatched her from the barrel and it was a case of 'Peter pays for Paul and Paul pays for all'. Claudia was Paul that day. We had underestimated my grandmother's keen instincts and in a matter of moments, saw the consequence of Claudia's failed attempt to evade her return and the evidence of her warning, *"When you ears hard, you does feel"*. As we stood there, shuffling our feet and casting furtive glances at each other, a quiet sense of guilt and camaraderie permeated our group.

On weekends and during the summer holiday which we simply called *"August holiday"*, Youkona and I assumed the roles of teachers. Our daily routine began early in the morning. We had breakfast and a refreshing bath, then ventured into the flower garden to start our classes. Sometimes we skipped having our bath and went straight to teaching. On such occasions, CB remarked she had never met any other teacher—besides us—who went to school without a bath, but her words went into one ear and out of the other. We discreetly borrowed purses from my cousin Whitney's room and her platform heels, which dug holes in the sand with every step and we embarked on our teaching journey.

BECOMING BOLDER WITH EVERY STEP

Our eager pupils consisted of approximately twenty plants meticulously arranged in rows and columns, resembling the desks and benches we were accustomed to in our school classrooms. Armed with a chalkboard and guided by CB's outdated Daily Word books, we covered various subjects, mirroring our school curriculum. English, mathematics, science, social studies, spelling, and dictation were all on our agenda. When our green students stumbled over their spelling we resorted to administering mild disciplinary measures, wielding a twig from the nearby guava tree or a wooden ruler. However, we had to exercise caution, for any off-target strike risked damaging a fragile stem, severing tender leaves, or denting a plant pot.

Our garden classes took place beneath the welcoming shade of the breadfruit tree in the back of our yard. We paused these sessions only temporarily when my grandmother's resonant call beckoned us inside for lunch. We dutifully dismissed our students and sent them home for lunch, even reciting the prayer we learnt at school. Then, our classes resumed promptly after we savoured our meal. Despite the garden being just a stone's throw away from our house, we often lingered on the wooden fence for much longer. Here, we indulged in a playful charade, imagining ourselves married to motorcycle-riding husbands who would drop us off at the *"bank"*—the budding jamun tree. In this whimsical scenario, we withdrew handfuls of imaginary money and stuffed our purses to the brim with the fictitious bills plucked from the tree's branches.

    When we weren't teaching and could rope in the boys from riding their bicycles, dissecting grasshoppers, or playing a spirited game of cricket, we operated a thriving restaurant business. The menu offered nothing short of an exquisite dining experience. The appetiser was a rich soup made with water, leaves and flowers. For the main course, there was an array of succulent, wild ginger as our meat, served alongside a bed of finely prepared sand that mimicked rice and a generous portion of vibrant foliage as our vegetable. Water was versatile enough to be any beverage our customer requested: bubbly champagne, wine or fruit juice. Then, to top it all off, the dessert was an exquisite, caramelised mud pie lovingly garnished with a freshly picked flower. Every expense was paid in jamun leaves. *"Yum, Yum"*, we delighted with each bite—slapping our tongues and rolling our eyes as if it was the best meal of our lives.

    As we grew older, our mischief moved to the pages of the book *'Growing Up'*. Little did Mommy know when she brought home that book it would unleash a new set of adventures for us. We playfully flipped through the pages with colourful illustrations depicting the mysteries of adolescence, but the pages that piqued our curiosity the most were the pages that held drawings of the anatomical changes. The book vividly portrayed the transformation awaiting us in our teenage years. We were captivated by the idea that boys would develop an Adam's apple and their voices would change remarkably, deepening into a more mature tone. For us girls, the book showed us it would be blossoming into womanhood with breasts and the grand entrance of the menstrual cycle. It all seemed so intriguing.

Sure, that was all fun and games until breasts started pushing out from my chest like seedlings in fertile ground. Gone were the days when I could bathe with the rest of my younger cousins at the water-filled drums in our yard and race up our back stairs in our birthday suits exclaiming, *"Who reach last is a big jackass!"*. Like my cousin Whitney and the adults, I bathed behind the closed bathroom door and wrapped myself with a towel before stepping outside.

It was a silent whisper from the book's pages, manifesting on my own body. In the blink of an eye, I went from watching my cousin fasten the hooks on her bras to securing the clips on mine. Later, when I confided in my friends about the need to wear an armour on my chest, they chuckled and shared their own tales of discoveries. Some had already received Mother Nature's monthly gift, which they said was their least favourite signal of adolescence. It was a bond formed in the shared experience of growing up, a journey of surprises. The book had served as our guide, but these moments of personal revelation marked our transition into the complex and intriguing world of adolescence.

At the peak of my holidays, I ate mangoes like they were going out of style and watched monkeys gracefully swing from the fruit trees in our backyard. I skilfully rode my bicycle down the hill with one hand or neither, and played with the water balloons my cousin Whitney gave to me. At times, my balloons took on different shapes. Some had five fingers and others were elongated and cylindrical. I remained blissfully unaware that these balloons were either latex gloves or condoms until Otis pointed it out.

Then, as the holiday winded down, drinking senna pod leaf tea and having my feet measured with a pointer—pulled from the broom that was made from coconut branches—were part of our end-of-summer rituals. My grandmother brewed senna leaves and served each of us a cup of the unsweetened laxative. If I managed to gulp it down quickly, I received a sprinkle of brown sugar to erase the bitter taste lingering in my mouth. Besides the distinctive aroma of the leaves, it gave us a good belly-wuk for the rest of the day. The pointer my grandmother used to measure my feet was tucked into a side pocket of her faithful black leather purse—it was that same pointer she took to the shoe store to buy the right size of shoes for school.

BECOMING BOLDER WITH EVERY STEP

I did not know then that every turn of the pedal on my blue bicycle marked a ride away from my youthful days. I carried my childhood adventures, which shaped me into the woman I have become. Those years of innocence, playfulness and curiosity evolved into the willingness to explore, take risks and find joy in the simplest things. No matter how complex and challenging life would become, there would always be a place for magic, mischief and my unbridled joy of curiosity. Right in those moments I continued to shape the adventures of my life one day at a time.

CHAPTER 4

Home and haven

My hometown, Bartica, sits on the bank of the Essequibo River between the Cuyuni and Mazaruni Rivers. The name Bartica itself means *'Red Earth'*, reflecting the rich natural beauty that surrounds this place. In this close-knit community that I call home, there has always been an undeniable sense that I'm connected to everyone—or at least, everyone knows who I am. These connections materialise when someone mentions that their grandmother was a distant cousin of my great-great-grandmother or exclaims, *"You is the splitting image of your mother!"* On the one hand, I couldn't do anything—whether good or bad—without it being reported to my parents. On the other hand, it's precisely those connections that define the very essence of home for me. It's the sense of belonging, the reassuring presence of familiar faces, and the comforting safety that comes from being in a place where I am recognised and embraced.

My grandmother's house perched proudly on wooden stilts atop a hill—it was my sanctuary of treasured memories and endless adventures. That same house passed down to CB from my great-grandmother, stood up against every storm. In my opinion, it was stronger than our neighbour's concrete house from which the wind once ripped the zinc sheets during a storm. The two bedrooms where we peeped through the cracks in the walls barely fit us. Yet those same rooms expanded to accommodate all my cousins who visited during the holidays. Within those humble wooden walls and creaking floorboards, I experienced the quintessential joys of childhood—the carefree days of running barefoot, getting bête rouge stuck to my skin and gleefully rolling in the grass and down hills.

Our yard was our canvas of imagination, playground, and refuge. We transformed into cricketers with our bat, ball and plastic drinks case—which we used as our wicket. We played hopscotch, skipped rope with unbridled enthusiasm, and ran wild while our breathless laughter filled the air. This shared space, blessed by the presence of fruit trees, was a realm where we revelled all day in the simple pleasures of our youth until the sunset signalled the end of our playtime and invited croaking frogs, candleflies, and mosquitos that were eager to eat us alive.

The coconut tree at the front gate stuck its neck high in the sky, and its unreachable bounty teased us mercilessly. By the time the coconuts fell to the ground, they were already dry. In addition to the coconut tree, the sugar apple tree stood as an accomplice in our grand adventures. We tied two pieces of rope to one of its sturdy branches and secured the loose ends to a piece of wood to fashion a makeshift swing. For us, each tree played a multifaceted role—not only did they bear fruits, but their leaves held the promise of prosperity, and their branches bore the weight of our youthfulness. In our backyard, kuru palms, bananas, mangoes, avocados, breadfruit, plum rose, cherries, cocoa pods, and golden apples flourished in abundance. There was a pawpaw tree too until my cousin, Jason, who visited during an August holiday attempted a Jack and the Beanstalk stunt—climbing the tree and completely uprooting it.

The cock-a-doodle-doo of CB's roosters was our daily alarm and morning signal. My grandmother, who was awake before sunrise, read her Holy Bible and ventured outside to open her chicken coops. For her, the sun rising while we slept was a sure sign of laziness. The Potaro Road, where we lived, was characterised by bad roads, shortcuts, and bushes, so it was not unusual to awaken and find prints left behind by a jaguar that had visited during the night and ravished the chicken coop. However, jaguars were not the only uninvited guests. When Keshauna was still a baby, there were mornings when we awoke and found large black-and-blue patches on her arms or legs that she didn't have the night before. Upon inspecting her tiny body, CB declared that it was the work of an Ole Higue and she rubbed down Keshauna nightly with cow gall from the abattoir.

While my grandmother remained uncertain about the identity of the Ole Higue, I was convinced by our neighbour's whispers that it was an elderly woman who lived a few houses up the road. Unlike CB, who didn't like listening to tales or entertaining gossip, our neighbour was like the antenna on our big back TV, picking up every village news and *seh seh*. I had no real proof that the woman turned into a ball of fire at night and flew into our home but I watched her like a hawk. I always suspected there was a story behind her freckly, wrinkled skin. Then, what made the matter worse was that she never said a word or greeted us when she passed. If she hoped her silence exonerated her, she was wasting her time. My mind was made up: she was the Ole Higue sucking my baby sister's blood at night and I secretly joined forces with CB to catch her.

I devised a plan to expose the bloodsucker and teach her a good lesson for flying into our home. Unknowing to my grandmother, I scooped up four or five handfuls of rice into a bowl. Before I went to bed each night, I positioned the bowl at the entry of our front door. As soon as the Ole Higue flew under the door—as I suspected she would, the bowl would stop her in her tracks. She would have to count every rice grain before proceeding to suck my baby sister, and if she only stumbled while counting, she would have to start again from the first grain. I was confident in my plan and certain that sunrise would catch her in distress counting the rice grains. As soon as sunrise came, she would burn out her skin, and I would catch her red-handed. But somehow, every morning when I awoke, there was only the bowl of rice grains I had placed the night before and no Ole Higue to be found.

I continued for weeks to set the trap at the entry of our doorway and await my impending victory at sunrise until the news of violence on the television screen drowned out everything. No one talked about the Ole Higue—neither CB nor our neighbour. When the 6 o'clock news came on, CB hushed us—telling us to put our fingers on our lips, so she could hear every word. When she stood at the fence to talk with Tr June, they only talked about things on the news and about some *'massacre'*. It was the first time I heard the word *'massacre'*, but it was connected to what was happening to the people on the news. Eavesdropping on CB's conversations always taught me new words.

In the same way that I listened to the news anchor's reports about the death squad and 2005 flood waters rising to people's necks and covering their homes, I watched the news of the massacre through the television. Big people and children were killed, and the people on the news bawled plenty eye-water. For many days after the massacre, I saw the faces of the people who died on the front page of the newspapers. The adults in the minibuses lamented over the heartlessness of the shooters and how they could never see God's face. My teachers at school bemoaned the deaths of the children around our age—their children and students. Mr Phurpo, an elderly man whose buttocks spread out like roti on a pan to cover both seats in the front of the minibus exclaimed, *"Bartica is a real blessed place!"* as he licked his fingertip to flip through the newspaper.

Watching the daily news and death announcement segment made the inside of my belly bubble like a pot of soup. To me, the only difference was that there were different songs during the death announcement segment, but John King's *"How Many More"* played with every news broadcast. Still, when I pressed the power button on the TV and switched back to my reality, there was no killing nor flooding—only minibus strikes, power outages and longing for more playtime.

February 17, 2008, was not a special day in our household. Like every other Sunday, I went to Sunday School—twice, then spent the afternoon playing hide and seek with my siblings and cousins. In the evening, cricket lovers set aside every other thing to rally around Guyana in the much anticipated T20 cricket quarter-final match against Antigua. Cricket, more than anything, has always united our people and brought out their all-rounded skills—directing the bowler how to knock the stumps or instructing the batsman to strategically hit the ball over the boundary for a *'clean six'*. Perhaps cricket is the only time when nobody talks about rich man or poor man or black man or coolie man. Instead, everyone becomes completely caught up in the thrill of the game—proudly waving the Golden Arrowhead and cheering from the stands, grass mounds or at the edge of their bed like Mommy and I.

My Secondary School Entrance Examination was less than a month away but on that particular Sunday night, I sat next to Mommy with my eyes glued to the TV instead of revising past examination papers. With Guyana having more runs to chase than available balls, the game could go in either of the team's favour. *"Lash the blasted ball!"*, Mommy shouted to the batsman who could not hear her. *"Damn it!"*, she exclaimed every time Guyana didn't score a run. Down to the final over, when Guyana was on the cusp of taking the T20 Title, a phone call shattered our tranquillity. My mother's cordial *"Hello"* quickly turned into shock with her widening eyes as she shifted focus from the TV screen. I could sense something was wrong. Mommy disconnected the call, then her fingers flew over the keypad as she dialled other numbers, which went unanswered before an incoming call came that I tuned my ears to hear.

BECOMING BOLDER WITH EVERY STEP

Our police station was attacked by gunmen who hijacked weapons, took ammunition and a patrol vehicle. Disguised as policemen, the gunmen rampaged through our community with high-powered rifles in search of only God knows who or what. In an instant, the violence that was once confined to the TV screen now threatened our very existence. Mommy hurriedly switched off the TV and the diesel generator that powered our home. I could hear a pin drop in the night and if we heard any approaching sounds, Mommy planned to hide me in the ceiling. I couldn't put my feelings in words but as the lights went off that night, the comforting safety of my hometown went along with it.

I lay still in the darkness beside Mommy, my heart pounding with dread as I wished her phone would stop ringing. The gunmen needed only to walk past her bedroom window for the light and sound from her cell phone to alert them of our presence. Thankfully, in the middle of my fear, sleep overtook me. But when morning came, twelve persons were slain—three policemen, six crew members of a docking vessel, two security guards and a taxi driver. One of the security guards, who also worked as a cobbler during the day, apparently ran out upon hearing the sounds at the police station and straight into his demise. The taxi driver and his friend were on their way home when their car was riddled with bullets. The driver died while his friend survived the attack, although the traumatic state in which he was left seemed like a worse fate.

I wondered what Mr Phurpo thought as he awoke to news of the Bartica Massacre on that day. I wondered if he still considered Bartica *"a real blessed place!"* The next day, I told Mommy that I could not miss school because our teacher had scheduled a mock examination. When I arrived at school, there was only my teacher and two other classmates. I should've listened to Mommy because I felt more afraid of the men returning with their big guns than I was afraid of missing my exams.

The song from the news broadcasts now played in my head over and over again. Every day felt like spiders were crawling in my chest and the fear of another massacre grew heavy. The stores that once opened late dropped their metal shutters long before sunset. The streets and corners where groups of friends usually lingered for an afternoon lime were as clean as a whistle. The shooting turned my hometown into a ghost town. It was as though everyone had been wounded by bullets—not just the victims, but every resident, carrying invisible scars of fear and suspicion. The residents became apprehensive about every strange face that showed up in our community. No one was caught or convicted for the murders as yet, which meant that the gunmen could have been living right under our noses.

Six months after the massacre, I graduated from Primary School and moved to the city. When my brother, Otis, left our home in Bartica two years prior, I looked forward to passing my exams with flying colours so I could join him, but the months that preceded my departure were far less than exciting. The stories on the news continued and when I pressed the power button, I still felt the dreadfulness and grief I'd been feeling since the night of the massacre.

The city was an exciting place to spend my holidays but when I moved there to live, I felt like it would swallow me up. Everything was bigger, more bustling and jam-packed than back home. Stabroek market, which I saw in my Social-Studies textbook and during my holidays was a massive maze and hub for minibuses and taxis. And as big as it was, there were as many vendors on the outside as on the inside. Passing by, I would be bombarded with vegetables thrust towards me, the vendors calling out, *"Aunty, wha you gah get today?"*. If I wasn't quick enough to indicate that I was neither an *"aunty"* nor shopping for anything, the vendor might push a plastic bag with eschallot in my hand while saying, *"Nice seasoning aunty, cheap and sweet!"*.

Unlike my friend's father who sold DVDs and CDs from his shop, the men who sold DVDs in the city encroached on the pavement with their full layout of pirated Bollywood, African moods, action films and every other genre of movies. CDs were sold like snow cones—men pushing their mobile carts blasting music through the streets. That was how the latest hits were advertised. Back home, there was just one spot where I easily caught a bus but in the city, I had to be ever cautious. The spot to take a bus home differed from the spot to take a bus to school. The bus parks in the city were where the best tug-of-war players competed. As soon as the touts saw someone approaching, they started pulling. If I didn't stand my ground and declare that I didn't want anyone to hassle me, one tout would try pulling me in the direction of his bus and another tout in the direction of his bus. Another observation I made in the city was that traffic rules didn't apply to minibuses; at least so it seemed. An amber light was simply an indication to drive faster while some bus drivers even drove through red lights like they were completely color-blind.

The stores in the city were gigantic. One store in the main shopping area was bigger than the entire shopping mall in Bartica. Since Otis was good at navigating his way around the city, I depended on him to take me wherever I needed to go. The problem with Otis being my GPS was that he was a one-stop shopper. Everything I needed had to be bought at one store. I, on the other hand, was enthralled by the enormous displays and variety offered so I wanted to go into every store even if I didn't need anything. Otis kept a vice grip on my hands whenever we went shopping on the weekends. With every trip, I mapped out my route so I could eventually go to the city centre and fatten my eyes unaccompanied by my brother.

Yet, in the same way that the city was exciting, it revealed its complexities. The colour of my skin, the texture of my hair and how I spoke became integral aspects of my identity. Back home in Bartica, I was a daughter—*Claudette Benn's granddaughter, Otis and Marcia's daughter, Pinche Bara's niece*—a familiar thread in the fabric of a tight-knit community. Yet, within the city's sprawling embrace, these elements of my appearance took on new significance, serving as markers that etched my unique story against its ever-changing backdrop. The revving engines and blaring horns replaced the rooster's crow.

I found myself navigating this unfamiliar landscape, seeking safety in the absence of my beloved grandmother, my friends and everything that had once been comforting and familiar. Many days, I yearned to return to the quiet haven of Bartica—to go out into our backyard and fill my bucket with kuru which I devoured with cassava bread, pick avocados, or swing from the mango tree—but the city was now my home and I had to adapt.

Despite their stark contrasts, these two worlds each held their own uniqueness, instilling invaluable lessons in resilience and adaptability. In Bartica, I learnt the importance of tradition and community. The close-knit relationships with our neighbours and the stories shared by my grandmother instilled in me a deep appreciation for my roots. In the city, I discovered the power of diversity and the richness it brought to life. I met people from all walks of life, each with their own story and background. The city's vibrancy and constant change pushed me out of my comfort zone, forcing me to evolve and adapt. It was in the city that I honed my ability to embrace change and thrive in unfamiliar territory.

In the end, it was these people and places that moulded me. They allowed me to find both a sense of home and haven in new and unexpected surroundings. I realised that home did not have to be confined to a single place. I would bloom wherever I was planted. The city had become an integral part of my story just as much as Bartica, and my identity had expanded to encompass both worlds.

BECOMING BOLDER WITH EVERY STEP

I will bloom where I am planted

CHAPTER 5

A monument more lasting than bronze

For the initial two years of Otis' stint at President's College, I remained a stranger to its grounds. It was Mommy who visited him. On the weekends, when he returned home, he told us stories about the pond which was shaped like the Guyana map and inhabited by caimans. He shared the excitement and challenges of adapting to the new living environment, making new friends from the length of Punta Playa to the Pakaraima mountains in the deep south, and about his adventures to the mysterious backdam which was an out-of-bounds area for students. I often daydreamed that one day I would attend President's College, too. I would escape to the backdam, milk cows, pluck chickens, see the pond, learn to speak multiple languages and play musical instruments. Thus, there and then, I made up my mind that I would be part of the Burnham legacy which he espoused to be more lasting than bronze.

At the end of June 2008, I received the results from my Secondary School Entrance Examinations and my journey to President's College began. Even with two marks less than Otis' score, I would still be joining him. All I could think of in the two months before I started my new school were the adventures ahead. On top of that, my friend Varsha would be joining her sister at President's College, too. I spent my August holiday immersed in laughter and adventure, making mischief with friends and creating memories at home but before I knew it, it was time to start my new school.

On our first drive to my new school, I recognised some of the villages' names from the news broadcasts. One village I particularly remembered for a riot where residents burned tyres in the middle of the road. But that bright Tuesday morning, the singing breeze felt like an oxymoron to those troubling news stories. Eventually, we reached the Golden Grove market square where there were taxi drivers lined up waiting for passengers, children full of chatter and laughter on their way to school, and women with voluptuous figures moving through the crowd; some had tables piled high with juicy mangoes along the road, while others balanced baskets on their heads like seasoned pros. Men on bicycles navigated their way to the back dam with beads of sweat already streaming down their faces.

When we finally turned off the main road onto the narrow street leading to the school's campus, I sat in the backseat of the car, still taking it all in. As the car approached the impressive metal gate with an equally impressive arch, the words that were immediately and indelibly imprinted upon me were **'PRESIDENT'S COLLEGE: SCHOOL OF EXCELLENCE'**. I could hardly believe that my dreams were really beginning to unfold. When the security officer beckoned us to proceed through the sprawling gates, my eyes were directed to the massive structures planted on the left, right and centre lined by coconut palms and bounded by wide trenches and stretched-out rice fields. I felt like I'd arrived.

However, as the road came to its end, the westernmost building in its architectural style suggested itself to me as the seat of authority and obviously my first pit stop. At the centre of the administrative building, it was almost made a sacred place where a massive portrait—twenty feet or so—of the school's founder and former President Linden Forbes Sampson Burnham hung above my head, exuding an aura of legacy and grandeur. As I stood directly in front of the painting, his eyes looked straight at me. Even as I walked to the left or the right, his gaze followed me like the moon in the night sky. It was as though he was affixed there, with his piercing stare, charging me with a national undertaking of excellence. Just a glance off from the portrait, there was a smaller wooden sculpture of him too, in a protective case, like he was looking from every angle.

The first day at President's College marked my entry into a whole new world. We stepped out of the Principal's office as files of students made their way through the administrative building en route to their classrooms and I heard some of them saying *"Look, there she is! Look Otis' sister!"*. Despite his apparent lack of enthusiasm and the exhaustive list of his twenty-five do's and don'ts he handed me a few weeks earlier, it was clear that my brother mentioned my arrival to his schoolmates.

In the days that followed, friendships sprouted easily as all the new students were temporarily placed in a single classroom. Our cheerful bonding was ever so often interrupted by the Home Economics teacher's admonishment that room 1 P was simply *"not a fish market"*. However, luckily for me, I sat on a bench beside soft-spoken Edrianna and vivacious Tandika who taught us both not just to weave intricate keychains but also colourful tales.

The following week we were all assigned to different classrooms and it was there that I met Enya. Eventually, our long strolls to the bus stop, shared and doubled rides in minibuses blasting the latest dancehall songs, and the modified transcribing of each other's homework solidified our bonds. Soon enough, we were branded the proverbial *"Batty and Po"*.

But this wasn't the only thing we did together. My friends and I were quick to nickname our teachers—even for the slightest inconvenience. We nicknamed one teacher *"Madam Bull Cow"* because she wrapped her braids like horns and another *"Sir Brains"* because of the size of his head. Our art teacher who was the strictest could rival Tina Turner with her impressive legs—but I wouldn't dare say that to her face—even as a compliment. Our Spanish teacher's crossed eyes made it impossible to even glance at my peer's paper during a test since I could never tell if he was looking straight at me or out the window. However, the Mathematics teacher was unlike any other. She was convinced that she could lay her hands and deliver us from every anti-mathematical demon that inevitably hindered the attainment of high scores on her tests. In her classes, prayers and prophecies outnumbered and rivalled the trigonometric formulas that she taught.

Then, the tables turned, and I became a victim of the same nicknaming. When our School's Track and Field Championship came around there were expectations that my performance would match Otis' athletic prowess. Among the institution's many traditions that honoured familial ties was the placement of siblings into the same sporting team, automatically placing me into team Diamond rather than one of the other equally competitive houses: Gold, Agate or Jasper. However, I wasn't cut out for the same events as Otis. While I could sprint a 100-metre race, the multiple laps and endless winding around the track which he seemed to inexplicably enjoy was simply not my forté.

More to the point though, in my most anticipated race, I entered the block, went on my mark, and shot off like a bullet at the sound of the gun. Only to realise upon raising my head, I ran off the track and into the crowd of spectators, placing last in the race and earning the nickname *"Big Runner"*. No year felt longer than the next to come around when I beat the national champion and wiped away the stain of my previous record.

In the year I joined Otis at President's College, we lived off-campus for a while before eventually moving into the dormitories. Needless to say, the transition to living on campus brought with it a unique set of challenges—the most difficult of which was coping with the constant water shortages. Most times, the pipes didn't run at full pressure, and we were forced to draw and fetch water from the back lobby of our dormitory. When those water tanks were exhausted we ventured out even further. Yet, as in one of the legendary Brer Anansi fables, the most clever of us found an invaluable solution in borrowing a bowl from everyone else's bucket so that we avoided the unenviable task.

Privacy became a luxury exchanged for the richness of shared experiences. The experience was one where up to three of us could seamlessly navigate the limited shower space to take our baths and get dressed by 7 am for breakfast. We were each adorned in purple kimonos, creme button-up shirts, and black shoes with white socks while our hair was neatly decorated with purple ribbons. The only exception was dressing in white T-shirts, sweatpants and sneakers when we had Physical Education classes. Our breakfast was quick as we returned to our dorms and got ready for the day ahead. This bit took the resemblance of the morning rush as we skimmed our timetables to pack our haversacks, smoothed any wrinkles from our bedsheets and neatened our cupboards before inspection by our house mistress. We made final touches to our hair, took one last look in the mirror and went through the doors for general assembly. Everything that initially felt foreign soon became intertwined with the everyday rhythm of my school life.

Lunch breaks found us standing in a semblance of a line, a routine that fostered camaraderie. Whoever was first to finish their class stood in the line to reserve spots for one, two or even six of us. Standing there, queuing up in anticipation of our meal with a moment of noisy chatter, feet tapping, and grudging stares as teachers walked in while we waited. The line was the longest on Valentine's Day when we had red and white rice with sweet and sour chicken or when chicken supreme was advertised on the menu. And if, by chance, the almost mechanical operation of lunching was interrupted by the sound of shattering ware, it was customary for the dining hall—endearingly called the D-hall—to break into enthusiastic applause, not in the least because the tortfeasor was a most brilliant idiot.

Evenings ushered in their own rituals. Sometimes, we disliked the meal served by D-hall and clandestinely prepared ramen noodles boiled in a percolator or pooled our monies for the occasional indulgence in Chinese food. The process of getting our food included pooling enough money to cover the meal, as well as the taxi fare to deliver the food. Then we walked from our dormitory to the security checkpoint and waited to collect it. If we had enough money, we added a bottle of Coca-Cola to our order. More orders made the process more economical. When our food arrived, it was serious mathematics to divide it based on the number of people and how much money each contributed—precisely calculating the pieces of fried chicken. After dinner, we had a ninety-minute study period where we spent the least time studying our schoolwork. If I didn't have homework to complete or a test coming up, it would be time spent exchanging scandalous notes of gossip and flirtation or babbling with my peers.

When our study period was over, we had time to mingle before heading upstairs to our dormitories. Those dormitory walls, witness to our triumphs, vulnerabilities, and playful indiscretions, nurtured a sense of community transcending geographical origins. Amidst the juggling act of work and play, there were clashes with the structured rules of the dorm. One such instance found us defying the *'lights-out'* regulation—driven by the relentless pursuit of excellence, or more so the impending deadlines that were hastened by Sir Brains' favourite thief of time—procrastination. Usually, this happened the night before an examination, a night steeped in the whispers of hastily exchanged notes and fervently revisiting of textbooks at ungodly hours. Yet, our resolve was to cram all our work into one night after prioritising recreation throughout the term. We huddled together, under the corridor's fluorescent lights poring over our notes. Occasionally, the after-hours chattering invited an impromptu midnight inspection from our unimpressed house mistress, who was ever keen to remind us that, *"Wha rain can't full, dew can't full"*. Her words were an allegory, a gentle reprimand wrapped in the profundity of Guyanese wisdom, cautioning against the folly of pursuing our goals at the expense of rest. But, despite all this profound knowledge, leisure could not wait and it was the same every test time.

Two nights out of the school year when we enjoyed not having to wear our casual clothes in the evenings or going to study period were Valentine's concert and Talent Royal: our version of America's Got Talent. On these two occasions, everyone decked out in their very best outfits—getting their makeup done and accessorising with costume jewellery, putting on balloon bottom dresses and high heels to strut down the catwalk on the imaginary red carpet that led to the D-hall. As we passed the male dormitory, our fans cheered us on. When our outfits didn't come together as we pictured, we mixed and matched pieces from our friends' collections.

At the end of the term, we took home our report cards. If I performed well, I excitedly handed mine to Mommy. If I didn't, I hid it from her until I ran out of excuses about not receiving it or lied about putting it in some long-forgotten place, perhaps akin to the paper bin. On the matter of performance, my mother and grandmother held differing perspectives. Mommy's philosophy was *'only the best is good enough'*, and that was her way—or as she'd often remind me, the *highway*—which probably meant somewhere homeless that I couldn't even fathom. Conversely, CB maintained an attitude of indifference to the actual percentages, asserting, *"As long as you tried your best"*, whether the results were ninety-nine percent or nine percent. In CB's eyes, my best effort was always good enough.

While being away from CB's reassuring presence was hard, my friends' parents became my surrogate parents. On Fridays, most of them went home and returned on Sunday afternoons. Kenia's mother, Aunty Doris, sent us extra pine tarts and cheese rolls when she baked pastries. Edrianna's mother, Aunty Kim, always prayed with us before we went into examinations. My first trip to Berbice on the weekend was a visit to Edrianna's home where, for the first time, I had the famous serving of Guyanese-style Fried Rice served in a brown pound paper bag, looking like something straight out of the 80s.

Our dormitories were not just spaces for living. As it turned out, they were also incubators of talent—from dancers to henna artists, elocutionists and impromptu locksmiths. The dormitory buzzed with diverse skills. However, the most sought-after talents during graduations and school parties were the hairstylists. The ability to transform our hair into intricate designs made these stylists stars among peers like me who couldn't even do a cornrow or flat twist. Stacyann was one of the stylists. Although the twists gave me a pounding headache afterwards, they were always a confidence booster. The finishing touch was standing in front of the mirror gelling down every out-of-place strand. I learnt from all those times I sat with my scalp on fire from the relaxer in my hair that *'pretty hurts'*.

The bonding experience between batchmates was intimate and enduring but age made a difference and sometimes that difference resulted in rivalry. Rivalries between jealous upper school girls over one of their male batchmates smitten with a girl from lower school. Those rivalries always stirred up feelings of validation on one side but contempt on the other side. The upper school girls sometimes referred to us as *'forced-ripe'* or pompous, and we labelled them *'wrong and strong'*. Although it was often between two persons, an offence against one person was, in reality, an offence against the entire friend's group; turning our molehills into mountains.

One afternoon, while we were outside having a grand time playing saul out, the upper school girls interrupted our game by teasing one of my friends about her dark complexion with a rusty made-up song. But, as the elders have always been keen to remind us, *"Do fa do nah obeah"*. In retaliation, we presented them with a graffitied wall of shame and shade. The graffitied wall was such a hit of notoriety that it not only provided the satisfactory embarrassment we envisioned, but also landed us in the Deputy Principal's office. Frustrated with our tit-for-tat exchanges, she mandated a public apology during the general assembly, forcing us to reconcile in the presence of enemies and fans.

Monday arrived, and we hoped the Deputy Principal had let it slide. Just as the assembly was wrapping up, she summoned us to apologise to each other. Caught off guard, we hastily searched for a blank page to tear from one of our notebooks. I stood at the podium, pretending to read the unprepared apology from a blank page feeling like the lead singer in the church choir, with my friends as backup singers behind me. When we returned to our dorm at midday, the nurse already knew what had happened.

Nothing happened on campus without reaching the nurse's ears. She was a slender woman with a brisk stride which suggested that she was always in a hurry to somewhere—even if that somewhere turned out to be the D-hall, a hundred meters away. The nurse knew everything about everyone—or at least, so she behaved. Visiting the sick bay for any ailment invariably led to a stern lecture like, *"You getting a fever because last night, when you supposed to go upstairs, you standing in the dew with that boy. You think I didn't see you, eh?"*

Regardless of whether or not I had truly been standing in the dew as she proffered, I learnt that it was better not to even attempt to refute her proposition because once she held on to a story, she held on to it tighter than a tick on a dog. Then, when she sat with the other ladies who worked in the school's laundry room, I was sure that she gossiped about us with them from their judgy stares as we passed them on our way to the general assembly.

Except for Mondays, when our general assembly was held in the D-hall, we queued up on the basketball court to recite our school's prayer and credo, sing our school's song and listen to any announcements. Reciting the credo renewed my commitment to strive for excellence.

We've come here to learn, while we're in our youth
To learn about life and living for truth

BECOMING BOLDER WITH EVERY STEP

To learn of Guyana – its rich heritage Of patriots and heroes of every age.

We've come here to learn, seeking for knowledge Here will we learn at President's College.

We've come here to learn, of Science and History
The thoughts of great thinkers who ponder life's mystery
We'll learn from experience how to be innovative
We'll learn independence, we'd also be creative.

We've come here to learn, to be not just scholastics
But also as farmers, athletes and gymnastics
We'll learn to be strong and fear not the future
We'll learn from our legends, folklore and culture.

We've come here to learn – we'll never give in At work or play striving always to win Whatever the score we must achieve fame For showing to all how to play the game.

All this will we learn as we seek here for knowledge All this will we learn at President's College.

WE CAN, WE MUST, WE WILL

The pride I felt uttering those words was the same pride I felt the morning I drove onto the school's campus for the first time. It was a reminder of the illuminating torch to be passed on to my sister, Youkona, and cousin, Claudia, who joined Otis and me at President's College.

As high school winded down, the chapters of dormitory life, shared experiences, and the wisdom imparted to me transcended the academic curriculum. It was a chronicle of growth, resilience, and the blossoming of friendships that weathered the storms of adolescence. It did not mark the end; instead, it was the transition into the next chapter. As we signed each other's yearbooks and made promises to meet up on the weekends, the excitement of newfound freedom and inching closer to realising our dreams made this transition easier.

Not everyone has the privilege of living with their friends, but I was fortunate enough to share this exceptional boarding experience at President's College. Its expansive grounds, diverse community and the inculcation of attitudes, knowledge and skills profoundly impacted my formative years. Long after I graduated from President's College, these words continue to resonate with me:

I can,
I must,
I will!

BECOMING BOLDER WITH EVERY STEP

Excellence
IS WITHIN MY REACH

CHAPTER 6

Checkpoint failure, destination success

We live in a globalised and hyperconnected era where filters, single angles and edited media obscure the realities of time and place. We spend hours every day consuming content curated to reflect a picture-perfect life. Our social media timeline is populated with people sharing their promotions when we've been terminated, scholarship awards when we've been rejected, and other feats while we wrestle our own battles. However, what we often don't see in the digital collages are the untold stories of resilience, the unfiltered moments of courage, and the beauty found within the messy, unscripted aspects of our lives.

Perhaps if we could do the same things that we see others enjoy or capture our perfect pictures and share them with the rest of the world, we might feel a greater sense of accomplishment. But the truth is life hits us hard and fast, and sometimes it feels like you're running downhill or worse—chasing the boy who annoyingly nicknamed you *"man voice"*. But before you know it, you've tumbled upside-down because your shoes are a size too big. Regardless of how small or grand the experience; the experience of failure is not unique to any of us. As I've heard CB repeatedly counsel, *"Rain don't fall at one man's door".*

We have all experienced failure somewhere along our journey. The world's greatest inventors, experts and athletes have failed many times before they succeeded. Thomas Edison made 1,000 unsuccessful attempts at his light bulb invention, J. K. Rowling's manuscript was rejected by more than twelve significant publications before Harry Potter and the Sorcerer's Stone was published and Michael Jordan recorded more than 9,000 missed shots in his basketball career and lost more than 300 games. Can you imagine what would have happened if Edison had given up after his first failed attempt, J.K Rowling had accepted rejection, or Michael Jordan had quit playing basketball after his first missed shot or even hundredth? They would have likely never made their mark in history.

Each example teaches us that failure is simply a checkpoint in our journey, not our destination. We can pause, restart, or take a completely different path to achieve our goals. As Denis Waitley puts it:

CHECKPOINT FAILURE, DESTINATION SUCCESS

> "Failure should be our teacher, not our undertaker. Failure is delay, not defeat. It is a temporary detour, not a dead end. Failure is something we can avoid only by saying nothing, doing nothing and being nothing".

As often as we experience failure, it allows us to assess where we are and determine what is required to advance to our desired destination. Yet, if we aren't deliberate about recognising that failure is simply a part of our journey, we can easily become overwhelmed, mortified or worse, paralysed. We may become convinced that no one can relate to or understand what we feel, our goals are not worth pursuing, or worse, we can't achieve them. Recognising failure as a checkpoint in our journey emboldens us to continue moving forward purposefully.

After completing high school, I enrolled at the University of Guyana to pursue a Diploma in Communication Studies. Upon completing the programme, I continued reading for my bachelor's degree and I dare say it was a turbulent journey. As best as I tried navigating this journey while balancing a full-time job and my entrepreneurial ventures, I was failing. I missed classes and assessment deadlines. I constantly writhed with my own insecurities and tried my best to ensure no one noticed. My grades declined from A's to solid B's, some C's and an F in the final semester. I'll never forget that I was sitting at my work desk when I received an email confirming my ineligibility to graduate that year. I clicked to read the email and immediately felt a rush of emotions—disappointment, regret and embarrassment. I closed the email, retreated to the restroom and cried my heart out. In many ways, that moment felt like it would change the trajectory of my life.

When I called my colleague, Keyshana, and told her what had happened, she was the one who reassured me that it was not the end of the world and that I could retake the course the following year. She even went as far as trying to comfort me by saying that I was luckier than some of my colleagues, who were graduating but had no success securing a job. Yet, as we stood on the rooftop of our office, I felt anything but lucky. I was crushed. All the little moments over the last four years, which were supposed to add up to the big moment of walking across the stage did not. Instead, they accumulated into a boulder of failure that came tumbling down on me.

I felt like I had let myself down and disappointed everyone. How was I going to tell my mother that I wasn't graduating after all her sacrifices? I had no idea how to break the news to her, especially since she was always the most excited about our graduations. By the time I got home, my eyes were puffy, and CB, who never missed a beat, followed me to my bedroom. As the tears started again, I told her what happened. She hugged me, planted a kiss on my cheek, and said, *"My granddaughter, don't worry. Everything gun be alright!"* Later that week, when I told Mommy, I emphasized, *"I'll go back and complete my studies next year,"* hoping my words would touch her soft spot. To my surprise, she was less disappointed than I imagined.

The next year came but I still hadn't yet mustered the courage to retake the course. Every thought of returning to the classroom was a dreadful reminder of my inability to achieve that goal. I filled the first year of being out of school with work, travelling, business and everything other than completing my degree. By the second year, I knew I had to make a decision. I could let another year come and go without completing my degree, or let go of the negative emotions I attached to this experience and learn from it. Reluctantly, I registered for classes and returned to complete the programme. Every time I set foot in the classroom, I reminded myself that every class took me closer to the finish line. On the day I received the email notification that I had fulfilled the requirements to graduate, I was sitting on my bed. I clicked to read the email and felt a new rush of emotions—happiness, pride and relief. I opened my journal to a blank page, wrote my first and last names, and then added my new credentials.

What I anticipated to be a four-year journey took six years due to turbulence, pit stops and every other hindrance conceivable under the sun. If I were to measure my success in reaction to that goal by only my ability to graduate in four years, I might still be wallowing in sorrow. Similarly, when we only measure our lives by our experiences of failure or the mistakes we've made, our existence can feel like a disastrous experiment. We see people from all walks of life take months or even years to accomplish their goals or take an entirely different path from the one on which they set out. Yet, as present and possible as failure is, so is success. These experiences remind us that success remains our birthright no matter how many delays, detours, or pit stops we encounter.

During my final presentation, my lecturer said she was happy I'd arrived at the end of the road, even though I *"faltered"*. When she said those words, they felt akin to packing salt into a gaping wound, but I only recall them as a reminder of my ability to succeed. I faltered along the journey, but failure was not my destination. The price for my success was all my pride's worth, persistence and perseverance. It was one of my most humbling experiences, and I discovered these five pavers installed on the road to success.

I. Availability is more valuable than ability.

We need more than our ability to guarantee our success. We must be present and ready to seize opportunities. More than that, we must be willing to persevere after we've encountered defeat. Our success requires us to be more than talented, clever or skilful. We need to be committed and available. As Angela Duckworth puts it: you've got to have 'grit'.

II. Procrastination is the thief of time

We often think that we have so much time available that we can defer things we need to do and squander valuable time that we could otherwise use productively. When we do this, we run the risk of missing deadlines and opportunities and altogether lessening our chances of success. Time is our most valuable resource, which we can never reclaim. The next hour, day, week or month will bring its own obstacles and opportunities. Now is the right time to do what needs to be done.

III. Every L is a Lesson

It may be hard to think that failure, as it is often crushing, can bring any good. But like the silver lining to every dark cloud, every experience of failure equally presents a learning opportunity. When we encounter difficulties or face failure, it's crucial to approach our situation with a growth mindset and a willingness to learn. Ultimately, it's not the setbacks that define us, but how we respond to them and the lessons we learn.

IV. We are responsible for our success.

We will never be able to control everything that happens but we can control our response to failure. We determine, by our actions, whether we will accept failure as our destination or recognise that failure is simply a checkpoint in our journey. We must take accountability for our efforts, learn from our failures and make necessary adjustments along the way. We are undoubtedly capable of reaching our destination, but we have to be determined to move beyond the checkpoint of failure.

V. Failure is not our identity.

Despite the number of times we experience failure and how often we feel like our life is a failed experiment, it is imperative to understand that we are much more than the sum of our failures and successes. Failure is a natural part of life; even the most successful people have experienced setbacks along their journey. Instead of dwelling on our setbacks or letting them define us, we can learn from our mistakes, adapt and persevere. While failure may be a part of our journey, it is not our identity.

Certainly, in a world with the impossibility of failing, we would dream bigger. However, the reality is that there is always the possibility of failure. In acknowledging this truth, we equip ourselves to get up more times than we stumble. We must be and do all we were created for and boldly live the dreams buried within us. When fear steps in, or failure occurs, know that neither is greater than you. Through all the trials and tribulations, we inch closer to our dreams, ever wiser, and ever more resilient. In the realm of possibility, failure is but a chapter, not the whole story.

BECOMING BOLDER WITH EVERY STEP

Success
IS MY BIRTHRIGHT

CHAPTER 7

A leap of faith, a load of courage

The journey from where we are to where we need to be requires a leap of faith and a load of courage. It requires surrendering our plans and the timelines we've set for ourselves and instead trusting our Creator to fulfil His purpose for our lives. Our journey also requires change. Like a caterpillar changes to become a butterfly, we must also change to become the best version of ourselves. We know that change is constant. Yet, we often resist change because it signals uncertainty, difference and discomfort, but change also represents growth, newness and transformation.

Ideally, we want to be sure that our lives will unfold how we've imagined. We would like to know whether the business idea that keeps us awake at night will succeed before we take the first step, if we'll be selected for the scholarship before we submit our application, or if we're going to lose weight before we start our gym membership. Altogether, there is an extreme level of comfort in certainty. However, if we stay put until we're sure that our journey will be all we imagine it to be, there's a big chance that we will spend the rest of our lives in the same spot—embracing comfort, but never becoming who we were created to be.

The Alchemist by Paulo Coelho is one of my favourite novels and reminds me of my own experiences, dreams, and aspirations. It is a beautiful narration about an Andalusian shepherd boy, Santiago, who dreamt that his treasures were buried at the Egyptian pyramids. The shepherd boy sold his flock to pursue his journey from his homeland to the pyramids. Along the way, Santiago loses all his money, meets a king and spends a year working for a crystal merchant. He was told that he could easily gather stones in his backyard and save himself a tumultuous journey, but the lad clung to his dream and continued through the desert in the middle of a tribal war. When he reached the oasis, Santiago contemplated how long it would take before finding his treasure.

Months went by before Santiago completed his journey. When he finally arrived at the pyramids, he sank his knees into the sands and began digging for his treasure but came up empty-handed. Instead, he was beaten and robbed by two men, one of whom mockingly told Santiago about his own dream of buried treasures in the sacristy of an abandoned church—the same church in which Santiago had his original dream. Santiago returned to Spain, dug beneath a sycamore tree where he slept and found his treasure.

I think that there's a Santiago in each of us. Along with the dreams buried within us, is also the power to manifest our dreams. In 2019, I reflected on some of my dreams while sitting on my bedroom floor. I had dreams of travelling the world and learning new languages. Yet, the longer I stayed at my work desk the further I stayed from realising those dreams and the stronger I felt an incessant and uncomfortable yearning for more.

While my job provided financial security, I had a gut feeling that I was missing something. Something more fulfilling than spending forty debilitating hours at a desk. Something necessary. Something worth pursuing, even if it took me halfway across the world, through the Saharan desert and at the feet of the Great Pyramids. As I mapped out my vision on a sheet of cardboard, I listed quitting my job, learning a new language and travelling the world.

In the centre of all my aspirations, I wrote the words:

'IF IT'S GOING TO BE, IT'S UP TO ME'

BECOMING BOLDER WITH EVERY STEP

That same evening, I drafted an undated resignation letter and began learning Spanish on Duolingo with two of my colleagues. I resigned by July of that year and left Guyana to pursue a solo backpacking adventure.

When I first announced my plans to my friends, some were ecstatic, while others thought I was losing my mind. *Have you gone crazy? Who are you travelling with? Who leaves their good good job to backpack? How are you going to earn money? What if this doesn't work out?*—I didn't know of anyone who had left their job to backpack. I didn't even know how I would earn while travelling. Not only that, but I was midway through my flight when I wondered what would happen if my plans didn't go as I imagined. I decided that in that case, I would return home. But when I came off the plane and saw my childhood friend and her fiancé awaiting me with their bright smiles and wide arms, I knew my adventure had only just begun. No matter where this journey would take me, I was ready to embrace it wholeheartedly.

I envisioned New York City to be just like I saw on TV- the Big Apple with towering glass buildings that kissed the sky and stores where I could choose from a million and one things. The iconic landmarks like the Empire State Building, Statue of Liberty, Times Square and Fifth Avenue which I saw in movies, were the things that fuelled my imagination. I pictured myself on shopping sprees and exploring until I was exhausted. However, I did not anticipate people asking me how I knew to speak English so well, 'cashless restaurants', and big rats scurrying through the subway.

After spending the Summer in New York City, I was ready for the next leg of my adventure. I joined Workaway—a platform that allows travel members to arrange work stays and exchange visits and connected with a hostel in Bogotá, Colombia. Through the program, volunteers or 'workawayers', contribute a pre-agreed amount of time per day in exchange for lodging and food, which their host provides. Despite the reservations of some of my family members and friends about solo travel to a country that spoke a language that was different from mine, I was ready to explore the Land of a Thousand Rhythms.

Then, two days before my flight, the hostel where I intended to stay indicated that they could no longer provide accommodation. As CB would say whenever she discovered money in her Bible, *"God don't come, but He does send"*. Zakiyah, a member of Workaway who was in Colombia, was God-sent. She reached out to see if I had made my way to Colombia safely and in no time we were making plans to secure new accommodation. Within a few hours, I was on the phone with Leonardo, who accepted my request to volunteer as a teacher at an English Institute.

At almost midnight when the aeroplane touched down on the runway in Bogotá, Colombia's capital, I went from the tarmac to the long travellers' queue holding my passport in one hand and the letter from Leonardo that I presented to the immigration officer in the other hand. Once I cleared immigration, I took a taxi to the hostel on the hill where Zakiyah awaited my arrival. A few days prior, we were strangers but now she was my friend, interpreter and compañero de viaje. Zakiyah paid the taxi driver in Colombian pesos, helped me carry my bag and we jumped straight into sweet conversations about how she was having the best time of her life in Colombia.

Bright and early the next day, we explored the colourful and vibrant La Candelaria in downtown Bogotá with astonishing colonial Spanish architecture and murals that adorned almost every wall. The rich aroma of arepas, empanadas and coffee filled the air and ripened my appetite. I saw beautiful carpets spread with clothing, jewellery, footwear and everything else up for a good bargain on the side of the streets. Dancers on stilts with their hips and skirts effortlessly swaying as people pushed past to make their way through the crowd, and artists who used coloured chalk to create picturesque drawings in the street. Vendors found themselves spots for their wooden carts loaded with fruits sliced and put in cups and others walked around with small bags that hung from their sticks, selling roasted Colombian ants in the same way that it was common to see the cotton candy man with his hanging bags back home. Even the little piggy that went to market was roasted and stuffed with rice, meat and peas into a delicious meal called 'Lechona'. When the sun hid her face and night descended, people and taxis made their way through less crowded streets. The lively rhythms of vallenato music awakened a different side of the city, with raised voices over Aguila beers escaping the open doors of bars as dance partners held on to each other.

On the second day, I was ready to climb Monseratte. I prepared for this adventure without Zakiyah, who had done it and warned me that it was not an easy feat. A short distance from the hostel, I made my way to the base like a pair of excited Guilder boots and purchased a cup of freshly squeezed tangerine juice from the man who already knew what I would soon discover about the mountain. The carved-out path started smoothly, but I quickly felt tingling in my feet as if I had stepped on needles, and my heartbeat raced like a town car. I could certainly use the oxygen that runners who passed me wearing oxygen masks were willingly depriving themselves. The smiles of descending climbers felt like nothing less than a mockery of my self-induced torture to trek the mountain instead of using the tram cars.

Seventy gruelling minutes later, I arrived at Monseratte's peak for the most breathtaking view of the city's landscape, and just in time for the mass conducted in the Catholic sanctuary on the mountaintop. *"El Padre, el Hijo y Espiritu Santo"*, were the few words I understood and repeated after the priest, crossing myself with the rest of the congregation and joining the queue to place an offering and receive the Holy Communion. When I descended the mountain, I was no better than a loppy dog with barely enough energy to make it back to the hostel. Thankfully, Zakiyah who knew I'd return tired, saved all the other activities we planned for the next day.

When I was done climbing Monseratte, zip lining and exploring Bogotá, it was time to make my way to Tunja— the biggest city in the heart of the Colombia Andean which hosts the most remaining Muisca architecture. Zakiyah followed me to the bus terminal, and we waved goodbye to each other. She was making her way to another part of Colombia to continue her adventures, while I was heading to Tunja to start mine. Two and a half hours after gazing through the window at the countryside, falling asleep and waking up, the bus pulled into Tunja's terminal.

"Buenas Noche, Señor", I greeted the taxi driver who assisted me in carrying my bag. I showed him the address Leonardo gave to me, he nodded and in less than five minutes, we pulled up to the apartment complex. I rang the buzzer and a couple also backpacking across South America greeted me. As God would have it, I arrived just in time for dinner and we shared our travel experiences over pasta and wine.

"LOS LÍMITES DE TU LENGUAJE SON LOS LÍMITES DE TU MUNDO"

In English, this phrase translates to, *"The limit of your language is the limit of your world"*. Those were the words of one of the first murals I saw on a wall right around the corner from our apartment in Tunja. Listening to the Spanish professors and Ceci, who prepared our meals, was nothing like listening to CB and Teacher June converse over our barbed wire fence. When I stepped outside to order food, I didn't recognise the words on the menu or know how to ask for what I wanted. When I asked Ceci to speak slower, she jokingly responded, *"No. Aprende más rápido!" No. Learn faster!* I had plunged into the pool's deep end and wondered what my high school Spanish teacher would think if she saw me—especially after I told her there was no need for me to learn Spanish.

When I wasn't teaching, I spent days walking to Plaza de Bolivar, noting words I saw on the shop fronts along the way. *Piernas. Brazos. Comida del dia. Ventas. Sopas.* Then, as soon as I returned to the apartment, I wrote the words in my notebook with the English translation beside them. Soon enough, I felt confident going to restaurants without the other volunteers who spoke Spanish fluently and sitting with Señor George, who had spent the last 14 years masterfully polishing shoes in the busy plaza. Like every Colombian I met, Señor

BECOMING BOLDER WITH EVERY STEP

George was happy to share stories of his life, city and country with me, as I was happy to share stories of mine.

I read storybooks and watched movies in Spanish; albeit with English subtitles. I eavesdropped on random conversations in the plaza and asked my students to teach me common Spanish phrases. Then, I thought, a word search puzzle would be ideal in helping to build my vocabulary so the next day I went to the bookshops in the plaza looking for *"el libro de búsqueda de palabras"*. After a few stops and people searching their brains like I was looking for something very strange, I knew my translation was incorrect, so I used a pen and piece of paper to draw a grid of letters and circled the letters when the shop attendant exclaimed, *"Ahh! El libro de sopa de letras!" The book of letter soup!* I would have never imagined.

Truly, time flies when you're having fun and I was having a whale of a time. I travelled to the nearby towns with the other volunteers. I was spending the weekend of March 16, in a town called Villa de Leyva visiting the fossil museum, casa terracotta—the largest ceramic in the world, drinking Aguila in the city's plaza and sharpening my Spanish-speaking skills when Ecuador unexpectedly announced its international border closure as a result of rising COVID-19 cases. Ecuador's announcement preceded airline flight cancellations, movement restrictions and panic as we were all flung into a state of despair. I packed my bag on Monday and prepared for a connecting flight to Guyana through Panama on Wednesday. However, before Wednesday arrived, Guyana promptly announced its border closure, restricting air travel, and ultimately cancelling my scheduled flight.

I missed the opportunity to return home in less than 24 hours. But like most people, I assumed that we would soon return to normalcy, the borders would reopen and I would be on my way home. Our classes became virtual. Days became weeks and weeks became months. Extended quarantine measures and new restrictions were implemented and the international borders remained indefinitely closed. I only left my apartment on the days that the last digit of my identification card permitted, and joined the long queues outside the supermarkets as people tried to stock up on their food supply.

Inevitably, the doom and gloom of the pandemic started to set in and even getting out of bed became an arduous task. Watching the news and reading articles about what was happening worldwide was heartbreaking; especially in the parts of the world where resources were already scarce. Some evenings, I heard loud clanking outside my window and upon looking out, there were groups of people—men, and women—some holding babies and children in search of food. That's how I met three orphaned siblings—Judy, Jesus, and Alberto, who stood outside the butchery asking for a piece of meat or some vegetables for their empty pots, which clanked against the haversack they carried.

As the months dragged on with no end in sight, my hope dwindled. There were new reported cases, a shortage of protective supplies and overcrowded hospitals. Whenever I could leave my apartment, I joined Leonardo and Manuel at their apartment. When they could leave theirs, we gathered for a movie night with pizza at my apartment. Their company turned out to be one of my biggest blessings. I still could not leave Colombia, but as the quarantine measures relaxed, Leo and Manu were happy to help me organise a trip to a farm in another town.

I was looking forward to a much-needed breath of fresh air. In the months that passed, I asked God for clarity about His plans concerning me. I missed my flight by just a few hours and ended up spending months stuck in Colombia during the pandemic, but I would wait for His response on the farm. In the week I planned to visit the farm, the institute could not find a replacement teacher, so I postponed my trip. When the following week came around, there was no transportation. By the time I sorted out transportation, my host had an emergency and just like the story of Solomon Grundy, that was the end of my going to the farm.

By this time I was frustrated but resumed my efforts. I contacted the US Embassy and multiple airlines hoping to secure a seat on one of their humanitarian flights. When the embassy finally responded to my email, the airline cautioned me: if I faced entry denial at the US border, they wouldn't assume responsibility or provide a refund, but this was a risk I was willing to take. Within a mere 48 hours, I had my first COVID test, hastily packed my belongings, and readied myself to embark on a flight from Bogotá to Miami.

On my drive to the airport, I took in the views and sounds of the city for the final time. It was unlike the busy city centre I flew into. The commercial banks and shopping malls stood shut behind large metal grill bars. Hostels, hotels and bars that once came alive were now desolate. There were no fruit stands, vendors, or dancers in the street. The pandemic had repainted the once colourful city in hues of blue and grey.

I hadn't experienced Colombia the way I planned. Yet, my experience was equally beautiful and life-altering. The previous eight months were nothing like I, or anyone, imagined. But I left Colombia knowing everything happened just as it was destined. In the same way the plane took off, I too, was taking flight for the next chapter of my life. All those experiences had prepared me and I didn't need to worry. I simply needed to remind myself that I was capable. The capability of the young woman who quit her job and left Guyana sixteen months prior. The power of the young woman who went to Colombia without a distinction between *'hermanos'* and *'hijos'* but left rolling her *r's* expertly. Certainly, that same capability would be enough to propel me towards what was ahead.

If I waited to accumulate a fortune before buying my first ticket, my dream of backpacking through South America may have still been just a dream. Likewise, If I waited to become fluent in Spanish before travelling to Colombia, I may have very well never flown across the Panama Canal and into Bogotá for the most life-changing experience. It was certainly a plethora of learning, unlearning, surrendering, and ultimately embracing God's plan. Looking back at the prayers I wrote in my journal during the pandemic, I recognise that my life became a reflection of those prayers. The greatest lesson this experience taught me was that we're not always going to have our lives figured out and sometimes, even when we think we do, we will have to create new plans when our existing plans fail. On our journey of becoming, we need faith to trust that clarity and wisdom will increase with every step, while courage prompts us to take the first step.

CHAPTER 8

Your gifts will make room for you

"Your gifts will make room for you", are not the words anyone wants to hear when trying to make space for themselves in an often confusing and complicated world. I'm confident of this because when my mentor, Claro, said them to me, I rolled my eyes and adamantly declared that I needed money to pay my bills; not gifts. Claro and I were catching up over a chai latte and some breadfruit fries. I was thrilled to share my victories with him. I started a new job, Stiletto Fetish—my women's retail shoes business—was expanding, and FruitGo—my fruit juice business—was supplying a new fast-food outlet. From eight a.m. to five p.m., I slipped into high-heeled shoes and behind my desk at work. Then, as soon as I got home, I stepped out of my heels and into my role as chief blender and bottler of FruitGo. Some things were chaotic in my life, but when it came to earning money, I had that under control—at least, in my opinion.

I shared every detail with Claro as I usually did and when I was finished, I expected to receive his approving grin. However, Claro leaned in, his eyes full of wisdom, and he said in a calm, confident tone; that he wanted me to stop hustling and start discovering my gifts. *"Your gifts will make room for you, Danie"*, he added. Claro's advice was rooted in his belief that discovering my gifts would help me to show up boldly, but I felt differently. I desired to travel the world, learn to speak different languages and enjoy my life without restrictions. All of those things required money. *Dinero!* Even so, I recorded his words in my journal that evening, and as unsure as I felt about how my gifts would make room for me, our conversation aroused a curiosity to discover what gifts I may have. Could talking be one of my gifts? Talking came easily and I did it all the time. After all, that was the reason CB nicknamed me *"Prattle Minister"*.

Sometimes, talking got me into trouble, though. There was one time when our school's Principal asked if anyone in our class witnessed a physical altercation between a parent and teacher. I was the only pupil who responded affirmatively. I'd seen the raging mother bolt across to the unsuspecting teacher in his classroom and delivered a slap which sent his glasses flying across the classroom. Later, when I was summoned to the principal's office and sat at a table with some people who acted like they were important with their recording devices, I recounted what I had seen. Little did I know, I had talked my way into big people's business.

Then I went on to high school, where I talked some more but not the talking that made me a witness or got me into trouble—all the time. I delivered the vote of thanks during guest visits, participated in debate and impromptu competitions, and often served as the delegated spokesperson among my peers. Beyond that, my role as the President of the Students' Council involved advocating for improved student resources and adherence to school rules. I took my role as President very seriously. Some of my peers even joked that I was like a police officer, going beyond my duties as a prefect, enforcing rules and maintaining order.

I also wondered if entrepreneurship was one of my gifts. Although my sticky-finger cousin had carted off our small jar of notes and coins, I enjoyed learning how to multiply my money. Whether that was rearing poultry and watching about one hundred or so broiler chickens eat their way to high market value or emptying my savings account to become a reseller of women's beauty products, my mother's shrewdness inspired me to start my own entrepreneurial ventures. Still, I was conflicted about whether entrepreneurship was a gift or merely a growing appetite for independence. In the months that followed dinner with Claro, there was an ever-growing insecurity from being unable to answer a question that no one else was more capable of answering. Eventually, when I felt like I just didn't have the answer, I found myself back at Claro, asking him what he thought were my gifts. And sure enough, by the time he was done, I was in no better position than when he first posed the question. Simply put, he said I was looking in the wrong place, and had to search within to discover my gifts.

Discovering Our Gifts.

We have all been given gifts and talents by our Creator to use in the fulfilment of His purpose. This is not only true for some of us but for all of us. In my final week at work, as I walked past one of my colleagues in the corridor, she said, *"I'll be looking out for your book"* and I responded with a crooked smile. Her remark was undeniably flattering, but I had no plans to write a book. I'd mapped out my journey and I was ready to explore the rest of the world. *Hasta Luego!*

When I left Guyana for my backpacking adventures, I continued to share stories on my blog. I shared stories about my travel experiences, my failed disguise from Limpy the minibus conductor and some lessons I learnt beyond the classroom. The more consistently I wrote, the easier writing became. Each story allowed me to connect with people from all over the world. I'd spent the last year learning from failure, redirection, and embracing every leg of my journey as it unfolded.

Even with my life being a far stretch from perfect and nowhere I imagined it to be, I resolved that telling stories that inspired others would suffice while I sought to discover my gifts. What began as sporadic blog posts became weekly anecdotes. Whenever I felt unsure of what story to tell, I whispered a prayer asking God to grant me the wisdom to write and the courage to share. Time and again, I heard Claro's words ringing in my ear and I pondered them until something else filled my thoughts. Then, one day, as I thought about his words, I realised I had found an answer.

Writing.

Writing was more than my hobby—it was one of my gifts. Whether I was writing in my journal about the friend I might have fallen in love with or telling stories on my blog, writing was one of the things that brought me joy. In hindsight, my blog wasn't birthed by accident, nor were any of the stories coincidental. The blog's name 'Learning, Being, Becoming: Daniella-Enough' catalogues the journey of discovering my gifts by discovering I am God's handiwork, created to do what he has prepared in advance. Each story was an opportunity to discover my gift and acknowledge that my gift was already within me; waiting to be discovered. It wasn't anything I didn't already possess or something I needed to look for in a distant or unknown place.

Every gift we have is already within us. They have been within us from the beginning. Thankfully, our Creator's desire is not for us to spend our lives in ignorance or confusion about who we are and why we were created. Not only has he given us our identity, but he has given us gifts and talents to do what he has created us to do. How, then, do we discover our gifts? We discover our gifts by seeking God and searching within ourselves.

Developing Our Gifts.
When we discover our gifts, we must develop them through practice. Developing what is already within us gives us clarity in our identity and the confidence to show up as our best selves. When we know who we are and we are confident that we were created for purpose, we can harness the power we possess. You are not an extraordinary artist, athlete, composer, entrepreneur, leader, mathematician, poet, singer and writer by accident. Nothing about our abilities is coincidental; our Creator is intentional.

The gifts we have are the tools we need to fulfil our purpose. To develop his gift, the artist must paint, the athlete must perform and the composer must write music. The entrepreneur must start the business, the leader must influence, the mathematician must calculate and the poet must create verses. The singer must sing, the writer must write and you must do what you were born to do, in the way only you can.

Discovering writing as one of my gifts gave me confidence in my capabilities and reaffirmed my purpose to serve others through storytelling. Beyond that, developing that gift replaced my hustle with purpose and yielded greater returns than any other investment. Discovering our gifts is knowing that a seed is planted within us; developing our gifts is nurturing that seed until it becomes a tree that bears fruits. Developing our gifts allows us to show up boldly. That is exactly what Claro meant that evening during dinner.

A Guaranteed Place In The World.

Regrettably, somewhere along our journey, fear, failure, guilt and prejudice have influenced our belief that we either have no gift or that our gifts and talents are without any value. That is perhaps why our minds are wired to believe that success is only possible in a traditional career path. Ask a Caribbean parent and they will likely concur. I've learnt that nothing could be further from the truth. Every one of us has gifts to do what we were created to do—which is our most valuable asset.

No matter how little you feel in this big world and at which end you find yourself, there is a guaranteed place for you when you discover and develop your gifts. We do not need to worry. We simply need to be confident and persistent. As we become more confident in who we are and work towards developing our gifts, we progress in becoming the best version of ourselves. We are the perfect vessels for our Creator to do His will, but the impact of discovering and developing our gifts extends far beyond our own lives. When we show up boldly, we show others that within ourselves, just about everything imaginable is also possible and that inspires them to do the same.

This book is the discovery of writing as one of my gifts. Its publication is developing that gift and knowing there is a place for my gift. When I shared my plans to write a book, a young man asked if I genuinely believed my book would become a bestseller. He asked, too, if there was any place for a writer in my country. I smiled and answered affirmatively to both of his questions.

After all, it was not long ago that I stood in the corridor wearing a crooked smile, completely oblivious that my solo backpacking adventure would turn out to be a journey of self-discovery, and that my gifts would create opportunities I never imagined. I am simply using my gifts to fulfil the task that God has entrusted to me. I have been excited to take the stories from the blog to the manuscript and, finally these pages. More than that, I am excited for you to discover your gifts, develop them and watch the world make room for you!

CHAPTER 9

Starting a business, building a brand

entrepreneurship
/ˌɒntrəprəˈnəːʃɪp/
noun
   the activity of setting up a business or businesses, taking on financial risks in the hope of profit.

Before I understood the meaning of entrepreneurship, who an entrepreneur was or what qualities one ought to possess, entrepreneurship to me was simply what my mother did and who she was. Like most women in my family, Mommy did not have a corporate job. She woke up at the crack of dawn each morning, or as the Guyanese say, *'before bird kiss 'e wife'*, loaded up her trolley and began her journey. She would travel around and about a million potholes, over hills, through gullies and wherever else, to find her buyers. And, if you know anything about Caribbean men, there was an almost never-ending demand for her stock of Packoo, Banga or Butterfish because they had to have their morning broth. It was good business, but hard in the sense that profits hardly seemed to match the Herculean effort that went into the distribution. She simultaneously managed her stall in the local market until later setting up retail businesses and gold mining operations across the country.

When I was around seven or eight, Mommy introduced me and my siblings to running a real business and generating profits. We sold aerated bottled drinks and store-bought chips to each other at home until we started our own marketing campaign by word of mouth. Buyers around our age from the primary school next door became our first outside customers. Other neighbours followed shortly.

We ran a tight ship with a strict credit policy because we simply couldn't play with the profits used to buy our candy at school. Sometimes, we would use profits for pocket money too. I have no idea how much profit our business generated. Yet, we continued until that cousin, with the cat-pawed sticky fingers, pulled a disappearing act in which he and all of our capital and profits—a jar full of small bills and coins—vanished into thin air.

My first solo entrepreneurial venture followed years later when I was in my senior year of high school. I stumbled upon a cramped Chinese-owned store during one of my usual weekend window-shopping walks in the city's commercial centre. The store didn't have fancy mannequin displays outside its door or salesgirls beckoning passersby like the other large stores surrounding it. Instead, there were glass cases and shelves stuffed with clothing, jewellery, and stationery supplies with barely enough space to stretch my arms. At first, their beaded bracelets caught my eye, but the neon-coloured hair combs set off my entrepreneurial alarm. I figured I could purchase the combs and resell them to my colleagues in the dormitory, where there was a never-ending shortage. Every morning as the clock struck closer to eight—when preparations for our daily assembly peaked—there was at least one student who either could not find or had forgotten their comb at home and I earned a threefold profit by meeting their demand.

I multiplied my money by investing it into what people needed. That was what Ms Claire & her partner, Whiskey, did with the fruits they sold from their rickety wooden stand under the shade of a jamun tree and what one of my houseparents did when she sold channa, plantain chips and pholourie from her apartment to hungry teenagers in the evenings. That is precisely what I did, selling hair combs and women's beauty products, rearing poultry and eventually starting my women's shoes retail business.

Starting a Business.

My women's retail shoes business started as an obsessive idea about selling women's shoes. I was 18 years old, enrolled at university and ready to be fabulously wealthy. At that time, it didn't bother me that I had not yet come up with a business name, plan or strategy. I hadn't considered, even for a split-second, the legal and tax implications of starting a business. Still, I delved into wholesale marketplaces, compiling a roster of potential suppliers and vendors in my trusty notebook and meticulously perusing shoe catalogues. Day and night, I looked for wholesale shoe vendors and negotiated with them to sell me less than their advertised minimum order quantity. I remained unwavering, despite lacking essential documents and capital for wholesale purchases. When my efforts with wholesalers didn't yield any success, I veered towards retail sources, forging ahead with full steam.

The first shipment with 15 pairs of shoes arrived in Guyana and put a spoke in my wheel. The duties and taxes attached to the shipment were through the roof—shattering my hopes of turning a profit. Right then, a realisation crystallised: If I was going to be successful at running my business, of which I had every intention, there was much to learn—starting with the foundational step of choosing a fitting business name. Again, I went straight to my notebook and wrote down possible names, but none truly felt like the right fit. It was an unexpected suggestion from my brother, Otis, who casually tossed out *"Stiletto Fetish"* while crossing the living room, and I knew that was the one.

Then I added the cherry on the cake, 'Get it or regret it'. After all, the choice was clear—get a pair of shoes from Stiletto Fetish, or regret the missed opportunity when they inevitably sold out. With this new identity, I created pages on social media platforms like Facebook and Instagram, rallying my friends and their connections to join and share my online presence. However, when the likes and reposts failed to convert into actual sales, it was necessary for a shift in strategy.

I packed the shoes into an oversized shopping bag, accompanied by a supportive friend turned chauffeur, and went from door to door in my hometown. I unpacked and displayed shoes for anyone showing the slightest interest. If luck was on my side, the shoes would fit like Cinderella's glass slipper, leading to instant purchases. When luck didn't favour me, I packed up and moved on, remaining unwavering in my pursuit until fortune smiled upon me once again.

Growing a Business.
The birth and incremental growth of Stiletto Fetish as a reputable retailer in the local market today has been an experience that is beyond my wildest imagination. What

initially started as a pursuit of financial gain has transformed into a mission that extends beyond profits to enrich the lives of the women I serve. This evolution from a desire for monetary success to a broader purpose has instrumentally shaped the growth and direction of my business.

With the arrival of my second shipment of shoes, my friend Racquel graciously offered to feature them in her boutique, and I accepted a full-time job. This allowed me to fulfil orders on demand and optimise my capital while simultaneously guaranteeing buyers upon the shoes' arrival. Every customer walked in with a mission—whether it was finding the perfect pair of shoes to match their unique style or seeking a boost of confidence to stride into uncharted territories. As I dedicated myself to fulfilling the distinct needs of my customers, their feedback became the driving force behind not just repeat purchases but also word-of-mouth referrals which propelled the growth of my business. In serving each need my business expanded, one satisfied customer at a time.

As the business diversified its inventory—incorporating a broader range of styles and sizes—I, too, evolved as an entrepreneur. The theories and principles of marketing and business communication I learnt during my university days seamlessly integrated into my own entrepreneurial journey. My role extended beyond solely procuring shoes to encompass marketing strategies, sales initiatives, and a continuous quest for knowledge. Each incoming shipment didn't just bring new inventory; it brought the need to broaden my knowledge base. Each arrival prompted me to dive deeper into understanding market trends, consumer preferences, and business strategies.

To fuel this hunger, I delved into a wealth of books that became my guide. Books such as Robert Kiyosaki's *Rich Dad, Poor Dad,* Tony Robbins' eye-opening reads like *Money Master The Game* and *Unshakeable,* Darren Hardy's insightful *Compound Effect,* and Richard Koch's illuminating *80/20 Rules* became my constant companions. These resources were not merely pages to me; they were gateways to understanding the intricate world of entrepreneurship. Podcasts were another way I immersed myself in the stories and wisdom shared by accomplished business leaders, absorbing their experiences and gleaning invaluable lessons. Their journeys and triumphs became my classroom, teaching me what I needed to know to emulate their success.

Still, amidst moments of pride, I also confronted the challenges of an expanding business and the importance of building a supportive team became evident. Building a team allowed me to focus on my strengths and relinquish the burden of managing all aspects of the business alone. Before shipping in commercial quantities, my friends generously offered to unbox and repack the shoes, effectively cutting down shipping costs. My golden girl, CB, kept track of my inventory and managed the delivery schedule better than any application or software. When faced with decisions and risks, I first turned to Mommy—her resilience and guidance have been an anchor throughout this journey.

When COVID-19 hit, I temporarily halted business but CB insisted that I continue advertising. *"People can't know you have shoes if you don't advertise them. Post the shoes on the Facebook, Dani"*, she encouraged me to stay proactive in promoting the business. Ultimately, that turned out to be a defining moment—a turning point in the business. When the designated delivery riders were unavailable, my siblings and friends swiftly took charge of the delivery, ensuring they reached our customers. As a result, our market presence extended far and wide, marking a significant surge in business growth.

Reflecting on those moments, it's clear that they were defining moments, shaping the trajectory of Stiletto Fetish. It was not a solo endeavour; it was a collaborative effort fueled by the unwavering support of many individuals. The success of Stiletto Fetish is a testament not only to my efforts but also to the collective belief and support of those who stood behind this vision.

Building a Brand.

While a business and brand are related, they are two distinct concepts. Our business involves the production, sale and provision of goods and services, or both, to customers. Our brand, on the other hand, represents the perception, reputation and identity of our product or service in the minds of consumers. This includes elements such as our business name, logo, design, messaging, positioning, and the overall experience associated with our product or service. Our brand is the unique identity and image our business creates in the market. We build our brand through our messaging, marketing efforts, customer interactions and the overall reputation of our business.

When I understood this distinction, my approach to brand development grew more intentional. It was no longer just about increasing sales and expanding market presence. My goal evolved into creating a brand that exuded boldness with every step. This shift necessitated a clear roadmap, delving beyond the physical aspects of rebranding. Revamping Stiletto Fetish's identity involved more than just a makeover of the logo and imagery. It entailed meticulously curating the brand's visuals, and crafting messages that exuded confidence, while ensuring a seamless customer experience. More than that, it required a shift in my own mindset, demanding clarity of purpose and authenticity in my endeavours.

BECOMING BOLDER WITH EVERY STEP

Building strong personal or professional brands rely heavily on clarity and authenticity in our messages and actions. Clarity helps us to define our vision and mission. It also helps us to understand what we want to accomplish and put our plan in motion to achieve those aspirations. For me, it meant fostering a community of bold, self-assured women, and empowering them to stride confidently toward their aspirations—within and beyond the shoes I provided.

Authenticity, on the other hand, nurtures trust between our brand and those we serve—be it clients, customers, or stakeholders. Our brand is not our persona in the digital space; it is who we are in real life. It is a reflection and extension of our values, beliefs and principles. Authenticity strengthens brand loyalty and fosters long-term relationships. Everything we hope to achieve can be built on the foundation of authenticity.

While entrepreneurship can be a rewarding journey, is not everybody's cup of tea. Some of us may discover our calling in different fields, and that's perfectly valid. However, an unwavering confidence in our potential to succeed is necessary for those who have a fire within for entrepreneurship.

Five lessons I've learnt as an entrepreneur are:

1. Begin where you are.

So many great ideas are buried within us that may never be manifested simply because we're waiting for perfection. We strive for the perfect business plan, product, packaging and pitch. Yet, in the end, we accomplish nothing. Since the first shipment of 15 pairs of shoes, Stiletto Fetish's inventory has grown to hundreds of styles. Don't wait for perfection or ideal circumstances to start your business. Begin where you are and perfect your products or services as you progress.

2. Build a strong foundation.

A strong business or brand can only be sustained on a strong foundation. Your business must be built to adapt to or withstand changing trends, economic volatility, technological innovation and social and demographic changes, among other factors. For aspiring or new entrepreneurs, completing a business plan, conducting market research and understanding the legal aspects of the business may all seem burdensome or even unnecessary. However, these are fundamental building blocks for starting and growing your business and building a successful brand.

3. Become a student of your industry.

As an entrepreneur, your business's growth is directly related to your personal growth and knowledge of your industry. Whether selling women's shoes, investing in real estate, creating luxury beauty products or curating tea blends, there is always something new to learn. Develop a passion for learning about your business and industry—read books, listen to podcasts, conduct research, network and seek out opportunities. Make it your goal to become wiser so that you will adjust, adapt and pivot as necessary.

4. Bet on yourself

If we're not willing to bet on our ideas, why should anyone else? Our journey as entrepreneurs is fraught with risks, and the biggest risk that we can take is to bet on ourselves. Certainly, it is an honour to be recognised by others, but we must be confident in our capability to succeed. We must believe in ourselves enough to wager—even if we're the only ones placing a bet on our side. When opportunities do not present themselves, we must seek to create them. Remember, the stakes might be high, but you are worth it.

5. Be resilient

In the presence of challenges, we must remain resilient. Our ability, as entrepreneurs, to navigate challenges, crises or setbacks strategically and successfully is crucial to the survival and evolution of our business or brand. Embracing the mindset that challenges are not just hurdles but opportunities to pivot is essential in the dynamic landscape of business and everything else we undertake.

CHAPTER 10

You are enough

As we navigate our journey, it is certainly not without challenges and obstacles that test our courage and willingness to step out of our cosy cocoons. However, through these moments of adversity, we blossom and become bolder individuals. Each step we take presents an opportunity to embrace our fears, expand our horizons and discover our true potential. Regrettably, along this journey, we often find ourselves trapped by feelings of inadequacy—believing we fall short in one way or another: not tall enough, not smart enough, not brave enough, not slender enough, and a myriad of other perceived shortcomings. I've had my fair share of those thoughts.

Reflecting on my journey—from the audacious decision to resign from my job and embarking on a solo backpacking adventure across South America—there's a huge disparity between what I imagined and how reality played out. I've often searched for the singular, defining moment—when there wasn't an ounce of fear or uncertainty so that I could take a leap into the unknown and not end up flat on my backside. However, such a moment did not exist for me. Rather, many moments amalgamated to mute my fear and deepen my conviction that I was created with a purpose and my Creator's plans are meant to prosper me, not to harm me. These myriad moments broadened the horizons of my world and taught me to embrace new ideas and experiences. During those same moments, I was uncovering my purpose and evolving into the bold woman I was meant to be.

    I was once listening to the late Dr Myles Munroe as he spoke about purpose. His analogy, which likened us to products the Creator assembles, resonated with me. He said that when we buy a defective product, we instinctively return it to the manufacturer. The reason we do this is simple. From the product's blueprint to its manual, no one knows a product better than the person who assembled it. The same goes for us. When we struggle with the mystery of our existence and how to live out our purpose, we must find our way back to our Creator. By referring to our Creator's manual, we can uncover our blueprint—gaining guidance, knowledge, or insight that provides a roadmap to our purpose and potential.

Contrary, when we are unsure of our Creator's plans concerning us, our existence can become a whirlwind of emotions. This turmoil breeds uncertainty, anxiety and unrest. Despite possessing love, power and discipline, we tiptoe apprehensively along our journey. We shy away from illuminating our brilliance—our innate gifts and talents—even though we are created to be the light of the world. We play a role much smaller than the one cast for us in a world where our destiny is to radiate, excel and manifest our divine attributes.

In the eloquent words of Marianne Williamson:

"Our deepest fear is not that we are inadequate. Our deepest fear is that we are powerful beyond measure. It is our light, not our darkness that most frightens us.

We ask ourselves,
'Who am I to be brilliant, gorgeous, talented, fabulous?' Actually, who are you not to be?

You are a child of God.
Your playing small does not serve the world.

There's nothing enlightened about shrinking so that other people won't feel insecure around you.

BECOMING BOLDER WITH EVERY STEP

We are all meant to shine, as children do.

We were born to make manifest the glory of God that is within us.

It's not just in some of us; it's in everyone. And as we let our own light shine, we unconsciously give other people permission to do the same.

As we're liberated from our own fear, our presence automatically liberates others."

We are capable of achieving every dream we've dreamt. The moment we decide to take our first step, we consciously or unconsciously, set our compass on a course of confidence, courage and determination. Each step builds on the one before it, pushing us to become bolder and more daring. This holds true whether we're pursuing career ascension, delving into entrepreneurship, nurturing our creative endeavours, or fostering personal relationships.

Our willingness to take calculated risks, learn from our experiences and grow through adversity propels us into deeper layers of self-discovery. By continuously challenging ourselves and embracing the discomfort of venturing into the unknown, we gain new insights and develop a steadfast belief in our abilities.

The months I spent in Colombia during the COVID-19 pandemic were the first time my life came to a complete halt. There was no hustle nor bustle. In the solace of my apartment, I had the opportunity to peel back layers of who I was, and what were my values and passions. Beyond that, I was forced to surrender my impatience and embrace God's plans. I dedicated a significant portion of my time to prayer and journaling, answering questions which I knew only I had the answers to.

Who am I?
What brings me joy and fulfilment?
What impact do I aspire to make on the world?
What legacy do I want to leave?

Answering these questions required introspection and vulnerability. Truthfully, it took a lot more courage and honesty than I fathomed. In this process, I uncovered aspects of my own insecurities, preconceived notions and misunderstandings. Not only were these personal realisations, but also perceptions I projected onto others.

In my prayers, I told God that if it was His will for me to be stuck in Colombia during the pandemic, I'd at least like to be privy to His plans. The absence of complete clarity was frustrating, as it often is when navigating uncertain paths. But we all must do the heart-work—that's the hard work. The heart-work gives us direction for our journey and aligns our actions with our purpose. When we are aligned with our purpose, the challenges become more than obstacles—they become opportunities for us to grow and learn. The heart-work keeps us grounded, while the hard work propels us forward, turning our dreams into achievements.

How do I approach writing a book centred on trusting divine timing? The answer lies in the lessons I've learnt about cultivating faith in divine timing. When I initially signed the contract for this book's publication, I set a goal to complete it within six months. However, as I pen these words, 24 months have passed. The span between then and now has been marked by a series of interruptions, diversions and obstacles that have shaped the course of my journey. At certain junctures, the approaching timelines seemed insurmountable and I openly expressed my frustration to my family and friends. During these conversations, they reminded me that I had a choice: I could choose to resist and struggle against the natural ebb and flow of life or surrender and trust that every delay was serving a purpose. Ultimately, I surrendered to the divine orchestration that operates beyond my understanding.

While trusting divine timing for our lives is necessary, it is not always straightforward. As human beings, we are wired to seek control and immediate results. We set goals, devise plans and work diligently towards achieving them.

However, this natural inclination for control clashes with the notion of leaving our destinies in God's hands. When faced with delays, detours, or disappointments, impatience often creeps in. We question why things aren't happening as quickly as we hoped, causing doubts about whether we're on the right path. As someone once said to me, *"I cannot spend my days on earth awaiting heavenly treasures. I must figure out my life now!"*

Trusting in divine timing humbles us by acknowledging our limited understanding. We're reminded that our perception of what's best for us may not align with the higher plan. In our eagerness for certain outcomes, we might unknowingly close ourselves off from the opportunities and blessings that arise from unexpected directions. Embracing humility invites us to relinquish our need for immediate gratification and to open ourselves to the gifts that await us in the divine timing of events. As we release our grip on the reins of control, we create space for grace to flow into our lives.

Perhaps the most challenging aspect of trusting divine timing is navigating delays and disappointment. When our prayers seem unanswered, our efforts unrewarded, or our dreams deferred, we grapple with feelings of frustration and sadness. We question whether our Creator hears us, or if there's a higher purpose behind our struggles. Our faith is tested in these moments and our willingness to trust in the unseen is challenged.

Trusting divine timing is an invitation to dance to the divine rhythm that pervades all creation. It is an acknowledgement that there exists a master conductor orchestrating the symphony of our lives. This conductor knows when to bring in the crescendos of success and when to allow the soft melodies of introspection. It really is an act of surrender, a testament to our faith and a journey of profound transformation that leads us to the crescendo of our own becoming.

There is nothing that can dim our light or diminish our inherent worth. All that we are learning, being and becoming serves us so that we can serve the world. During moments of fear, failure, or uncertainty, we must remember that our source is unlimited. We can pause and rest, stop and start, fall and rise, and explore and rediscover ourselves as often as we need. In all these things, we can find comfort in knowing that we are enough. More than that, when we recognise that we are complete, we do not seek to compete. Instead, we become confident that our Creator who knows the beginning from the end will complete what was started in us.

As this chapter draws to an end and you step into the uncharted territory of the next phase, let go of the grip of fear, discover your unique gifts and talents, and wholeheartedly embrace the bold individual you are destined to become. Carry with you this unwavering truth:

You are enough as you have always been and will always be!

BECOMING BOLDER WITH EVERY STEP

This page is for you to write your next BOLD moves.

_____

_____

_____

_____

_____

_____

_____

_____

_____